Solution Talk

Hosting Therapeutic Conversations

Solution Talk

Hosting Therapeutic Conversations

Ben Furman

Tapani Ahola

W.W. NORTON & COMPANY • *NEW YORK* • *LONDON*

Printed in the United States of America.

First Edition

The text of this book was composed in New Century Textbook.
Composition by Bytheway Typesetting Services, Inc.
Manufacturing by Haddon Craftsmen, Inc.

Library of Congress Cataloging in Publication Data

Furman, Ben.
    Solution talk : hosting therapeutic conversations / Ben Furman
and Tapani Ahola.
        p.   cm.
    "A Norton professional book."
    Includes bibliographical references.
    ISBN 0-393-70135-2
    1. Solution-focused therapy.   I. Ahola, Tapani.   II. Title.
    [DNLM: 1. Communications.   2. Physician-Patient Relations.
3. Psychotherapy – methods.   WM 420 F986s]
    RC489.S65F87n   1992
    616.89′14 – dc20
    DNLM/DLC
    for Library of Congress   91-45316   CIP

W.W. Norton & Company, Inc., 500 Fifth Avenue, New York, N.Y. 10110
W.W. Norton & Company, Ltd., 10 Coptic Street, London WC1A 1PU

            1   2   3   4   5   6   7   8   9   0

FOREWORD

Perhaps I shouldn't reveal it (especially in this era when the word "politics" has such a bad connotation), but I believe that the practices invited by this challenging book go beyond being transformative at the level of the individual (familial) patient: They constitute a strong, progressive, political activity. At a certain level, therapy is always political. This is radical politics at its best.

Family therapy, and, broadly speaking, systemic brief therapies, had, as it is well-known, a multitudinous and rather famous ancestry: cybernetics, general systems theory, field theory, game theory, psychoanalytic object relations theory, and communication theory, to name but the most frequently recognized contributors to the genome of the discipline. But from this list is missing another parent, who has been less sung or who, perhaps, in this Reagan (and post-Reagan!) era of self-started individualism, has cautiously shied away from the limelight: I am referring to the progressive political movement of the fifties and sixties. In the field of mental health, this movement triggered, as a spinoff of community-sensitive activism, the revision of many practices and, above all, the deinstitutionalization reform (or was it revolution?), carrying as a banner the romantic passion of anti-psychiatry and the rhetoric and practice of social empowerment and social justice.

This root, forgotten as it may be, permeated the early years of the field. From its beginning, in fact, family therapy was heralded as a radical alternative to the established traditions of mainstream practices – the only quarrel being with the word "therapy," which carried with it the oppressive echo of too many years of authoritarian *fiat*. Ronald Laing and David Cooper – two of the most powerful exponents of the anti-psychiatric movement – not only were experimenting with medication-free, restraint-free, alternative environments for severely disturbed patients but were "thinking and doing family" – even when Cooper was writing *The Death of the Family*. In the U.S., Israel Zwerling and his group of mavericks – Albert Scheflen being one of its creative ideologues, Chris Beels one of its steady actors, Mony Elkaim one of their passionate students – were turning upside down traditional psychiatric institutions. They transformed Bronx State Hospital from a self-serving, socially disconnected institution into a family-oriented, community-based organization, demystifying practices and empowering patients. Dick Auerswald and his group did likewise at Gouverneur Hospital in New York. On a different front, Nathan Ackerman was poking at the psychoanalytic monolith with ana-thematic interpersonal stances, while other daring thinkers – Lyman Wynne, Margaret Singer, Murray Bowen – were challenging psychiatry in its own territory, the National Institute of Mental Health. On the west coast, under the intellectual guidance of Gregory Bateson, the strong anti-establishment stances of Jay Haley and the heterodox views of Don D. Jackson were being articulated into seminal ideas for the whole field. In turn, Laing, Cooper, Scheflen, and many other radical thinkers visited at one time or another Bateson's research team and its heir, the Mental Research Institute, exchanging notes and leaving, in turn, important marks in its key members. During that same period, in a low-key fashion, the "Soteria" experiment, under Alma Zito Menn and Loren Mosher, was daringly replicating in California the key tenets of the Laing group.

For all of them and so many others, that new, non-violent, non-intrusive, demystifying, collaborative approach-in-progress, *family therapy* was the reasonable alternative. And they were not just "using a clinical tool." They were, in fact, participating in the development of a model and a practice that was sensitive to basic human rights and to strong social concerns.

As time has passed, three concurrent developments have taken place. First, the local level of the discipline, family therapy has been busy mainstreaming itself and therefore has (had to?) leave behind its radical roots. Second, the systemic view has progressively reduced its dependence on models and language "imported" from other fields, as it has generated its own paradigm and lexicon and developed its own conceptual identity. In the process, it has entered into a developmental stage of self-centeredness, somehow distancing itself from its psychosocial and political roots, rhetoric, and practices (two notable exceptions are the feminist voice, which kept the political flame burning brightly, and the practitioners at the interdisciplinary frontier, who retained a countercultural, pioneering creativity and fervor). Third, at the background level of dominant ideologies, a worldwide deradicalization (perhaps with some populist exceptions) has been seen, at least in the U.S., in an overall swing to the right that increasingly threatens the hard-won gains of women, children, and minorities. The prevalence of callous, pragmatic, hands-off approaches to politics, resulting in a major dismantling of social and health-related programs, has turned social activism into a bad word.

However, as oscillations go, in consonance with what is happening in many other disciplines, a shift in the opposite direction is beginning in the field of systemic therapies. It appears with a different facade, low in rhetoric and high in revolutionary practices, faithful to the motto *Think globally; act locally!* It is focused on a dramatic shift in the micro-politics of the patient-provider relationship, a major revision of the basic tenets of the therapeutic contract and the therapeutic task. This shift has extremely important transformative consequences on the way patients (and providers) interact with their world as responsible agents of change, rather than as passive or oppressed victims of their fate or as dependent appendices of their therapists (or their institutions). This shift—characterized by a demystifying attitude of respectful collaboration in the therapeutic endeavor, by a stance toward expert knowledge on the part of the therapist that bars oppression and enhances authorship on the part of the patients, by a context-based view of problems and predicaments that increases people's own alternative options and responsibility – is superbly represented by Furman and Ahola's *Solution Talk: Hosting Therapeutic Conversations.*

Ultimately, what a lucid title! "Solution talk" orients us to the authors' strong epistemological stance: "Problems" (conflicts, symptoms, difficulties) are problems *in language*, that is, they are caught, retained, and maintained through formulations that seal off alternatives, preclude ways out, rob authorship. The riddle of the problem can be solved not from within its formulation, but through a back door which opens to new ways of describing it: the exploration of novel solutions. The lucid dictum "The solution constitutes the problem," which guided the first, crucial steps of brief therapy as formulated by the pioneering MRI team, is a reminder that whatever solution may have been already attempted by those consulting has, in turn, sealed off, retained, maintained the problem (otherwise they wouldn't consult!). Thus, the original, counterintuitive solutions generated in the course of the therapeutic dialogue *necessarily* imply new, original, counterintuitive descriptions of the problem, descriptions that effectively unseal the until-then self-fulfilling, self-perpetuating predicament that generated the consultation.

"Hosting" alludes to still another key notion: Therapists do not "do therapy to" the patient; they invite reflections, favor the generation of alternatives, open doors for new views, at all times respectfully empowering their interlocutor. The patient/client not only will find his or her own self-generated Ariadne's thread to guide him or herself out of their labyrinth, but will also *own* it. And where does all this take place? In the shared time/space of "Conversations," the common territory of language-in-action, the locus of consensus.

To practice therapy in this way is transformative for the therapist. But I do not want to rob you, the reader, of the pleasure of that discovery. Only a forewarning: Be ready for the important repercussions of your transformation. If you are working in a traditional institution, this practice has the potential to challenge the way patients are talked to, talked about, processed, diagnosed, catalogued, and charted; in sum, it will challenge the way the institution operates, pushing for a more patient-oriented and community-oriented orientation, for deceptively simple democratic procedures (with patients and among staff), for a new sensitivity to all forms of oppression and violence—especially those unwittingly favored by ourselves. To practice in this way would be transformative for the patients too: The new quality of the therapeutic encounter, through modeling if not through conversion, would affect the way *they* themselves interface with us, with their families, and with their institutions, sensitizing them to oppression and violence, making them more responsible and responsive characters in their own life. That is why I stated at the beginning that this is a profoundly political book.

In addition to all the above, *Solution Talk* is extremely wise, clear, useful, creative, intellectually invigorating and, as if that weren't enough, fun to read. This book legitimizes Furman and Ahola as inhabitants of the recently claimed, scarcely charted, and highly charged territory that lies in the confluence of narrative-based approaches to change and systemic brief therapy, and adds them with honors to the short list of key authors in the latter field.

Carlos E. Sluzki, M.D.
Chairman,
Department of Psychiatry and Behavioral Sciences
Berkshire Medical Center
Pittsfield, Massachusetts

CONTENTS

ACKNOWLEDGMENTS

We were originally introduced to the ideas of brief therapy and the legacy of Milton H. Erickson (Haley, 1973), the forerunner of modern brief therapy, through pastor John Fryckman from San Francisco. John first lectured in Finland in the early seventies and after that continued to visit and teach professionals here over a period lasting almost a decade. We have maintained close contact with John over the years and we continue to have high regard for him as a teacher and a friend.

Since first learning about this "different" approach to helping people with problems we have been influenced by numerous people in the field. In the early years of his specialization in psychiatry, Ben participated in a training seminar in Italy held by Luigi Boscolo and Gianfranco Cecchin, teachers of the well-known Milan model of systemic family therapy. On several subsequent occasions we have taken part in lectures and workshops given by these teachers. We like to think that the spirit of Milan systemic therapy, specifically the underlying constructivist philosophy and the pursuit of positive ways of looking at things (e.g., Boscolo, Cecchin, Hoffman, & Penn, 1988) has become an essential element of our way of thinking.

When we started training professionals in the mid-eighties at the Brief Therapy Center of the Mannerheim League for Child Welfare, we drew a great deal on the ideas of the brief therapy team at the Mental Research Institute in Palo Alto: Paul Watzlawick, John Weakland, and Richard Fisch among others. The team's book, *The Tactics of Change* (Fisch,

Weakland, & Segal, 1982) was a handbook we consulted frequently in the early phases of our work. Some years later John Weakland was invited to Finland. Clearly and with a great sense of humor, he conveyed the elegance of brief therapy at the MRI.

In the early phases of our work we also adopted many ideas from strategic therapy as described by Jay Haley and Cloé Madanes, co-directors of the Family Therapy Institute of Washington, DC. *Strategic Family Therapy* (Madanes, 1981) and *Behind the One-Way Mirror* (Madanes, 1984) had a great impact on us. One of the first foreign guests invited to Finland by the Brief Therapy Center was Judith Mazza, Ph.D., who was at that time the clinical director of the Family Therapy Institute of Washington. Her amiable presence and marvelous interventions (see Mazza, 1984) inspired us greatly.

Among our first foreign guests were Peter Lang and Martin Little, co-directors of the Kensington Consultation Centre in London. They helped us to see that the concept of a "client" should include not only the troubled person with or without the family, but also those well-meaning professionals involved in the case. We are indebted to Peter and Martin for helping us broaden our perspective from the nuclear family towards a more flexible network orientation.

Carlos Sluzki, director of the Berkshire Medical Center in Pittsfield, Massachusetts, and editor of the journal *Family Process* at the time of his visit to Finland, coached us in systemic thinking and conducted two unforgettable live interviews. He was the first to encourage us to translate our ideas into English in order to present them to an international audience. His continuing support resulted in our decision to write this book.

We had read with great interest the works of Karl Tomm, professor of psychiatry from Calgary (e.g., Tomm, 1987a 1987b, 1988), before we finally had the chance to meet him in person in Canada, and then again in Finland. He has inspired us through his willingness to engage in sustained debates about the philosophy of therapy, often until the early hours of the morning.

Bill O'Hanlon from Omaha, Nebraska, international teacher of Ericksonian brief therapy, finally helped us to bring together the concept of solution-oriented therapy. He encouraged us to leave out discussions about the hypothesis of the causes or functions of problems and instead simply focus on solutions (O'Hanlon & Weiner-Davis, 1989). He brought home to us the value of true collaboration with clients and launched us on our present course. Inadvertently, Bill also supported us in our decision to give up the one-way mirror and invite our clients to sit together with us in the same room throughout sessions.

Soon after meeting Bill we began to realize the significance of the work of Steve de Shazer, Insoo Kim Berg and their team at the Brief Family Therapy Center in Milwaukee (de Shazer, 1985, 1988, 1991). We have since incorporated many of the ideas of this team into our own work, as is evident particularly in the chapters "Future Visions" and "Improvement and Progress" (de Shazer et al., 1986; Weiner-Davis, de Shazer, & Gingerich, 1987). In recent years, as Steve, Insoo, and also Elam Nunnally have taught in Finland on several occasions, we have learned to respect them as truly original innovators in the field of psychotherapy.

Frank Farrelly, originator of what he has titled "provocative therapy," was undoubtedly one of our most amusing guests. We value his style of doing therapy, which is based on abolishing shame through humor, affectionate banter, and teasing. As we had anticipated on the basis of his book, *Provocative Therapy* (Farrelly & Brandsma, 1974), Frank Farrelly proved to be a true master of this delicate art. It is largely thanks to him that we have become so conscientious about working in ways that help people free themselves from both the burdens of shame and the fear of losing face.

At one of the big conferences on hypnosis and Ericksonian psychotherapy in Phoenix, Arizona, we heard a wonderful presentation entitled "The Use of Humor in Strategic Family Therapy," by Richard Belson, a former Rabbi who is currently working in private practice as a family therapist on Long Island. We invited him to teach in Finland the following year. Richard is still remembered affectionately by many people here. We like to think of ourselves as funny, but we have to admit that he is even funnier.

Many years ago, at an international family therapy congress in Tel Aviv, Ben met Baruch Schulem, a great story teller and Ericksonian brief therapist from Jerusalem who is also an orthodox Jew. His sparkling humor and healing stories had a powerful effect on his audience (Schulem, 1988). When Baruch visited Finland many years later, he managed to remind us of the fact that most, if not all, of our most cherished bright ideas originated in biblical times and even earlier.

In more recent years we have been inspired by the work of Michael White in Australia (White, 1990) and David Epston in New Zealand (Epston, 1990). Michael has described in his writings a charming idea that he refers to as "externalizing the problem." This idea has much in common with native healing and involves considering human problems as independent of people and their relationships. Externalizing problems is but one of many new ideas emanating from the southern hemisphere, where Michael and David have collaborated for several years (White & Epston, 1990).

It should be said that we have appropriated the phrase "solution talk," the title of this book, from David Epston. In one of his letters to us he wrote, "Solution talk is a phrase I have often used to distinguish between what I call 'problem talk.' I was once supervising a social worker who was attending a grand round in a psychiatric hospital and who was bored out of his mind. I suggested he use his time to research the extent to which those attending used 'problem' versus 'solution' talk." David's letter included a reproduction of a graph made by the social worker. It showed that 99% of the time the conversation involved 100% problem talk as compared to 0% solution talk. The one percent of solution talk occurred when towards the end of the meeting someone had come into the room and uttered the words "tea is being served."

We have had the pleasure of corresponding for a number of years with Lynn Hoffman who is a great synthesizer of systemic thinking. Through her letters we have become familiar with the work of many therapists who maintain similar ideas to those of ours. These include Harlene Anderson and Harold Goolishian in Galveston, Peggy Penn and Marcia Sheinberg in New York, and Tom Andersen in Tromsö, Norway. We value this group for their emphasis on the significance of language, and their high regard for openness and respect for clients.

We express gratitude to our clients, trainees, and all those people who have invited us to conduct workshops in our own country as well as abroad. We are also indebted to the many Finnish colleagues with whom we have studied, taught, and debated over the years. These include Kalervo Kinanen, Finnish-born professor of social work at Mc Master University in Hamilton, Canada, who was a pioneering teacher of family therapy in Finland and who seeded in our minds the idea of the importance of direct, honest, and open communication; K. E. Lanu, professor and late director of the A-Clinic Foundation, whose many original ideas have been a source of inspiration to Tapani; Reijo Junnola, psychologist and long-time friend, who has the expertise to justify the principles of solution-orientation from within any of the existing psychological theories; Ritva Saarelainen, teacher of family therapy at the A-Clinic Foundation, who has continuously supported and encouraged us in our work.

We have been fortunate to have as supervisors over the years people who have taught us to challenge conventional wisdom and encouraged us in our search for alternatives. These people include psychologists Pirkko Siltala and Helena Lounavaara-Rintala, and psychiatrists Heimo Salminen, Katriina Kuusi, and Kalevi Nieminen. We are also indebted to those solution-minded colleagues and friends with whom we currently collaborate: Kimmo Karkia, Eero Riikonen, Sara Vataja, and Katriina Pajupuro.

Special thanks go to our administrator at the Mannerheim League for Child Welfare, program director Toivo Rönkä, program chief Marjatta Jakobson, researcher Mikko Makkonen, and manager of training Pirjo Nuotio. Without their invitation for us to become the teachers for the brief therapy training program they founded and their constant encouragement over the years we taught at the center, there would have been no "fall of the wall."

Finally, we thank our editor, Susan E. Barrows, who has shown a natural gift of solution talk by her constant encouragement and kind advice; our dear friend Tiina Tarkkanen for her thorough criticism on the manuscript, and Rick McArthur, our English friend, who labored with us on many nights helping us express our ideas clearly.

INTRODUCTION

A woman met a friend of hers and began to complain about the unfriendliness of the local pharmacist. She said that the pharmacist was the rudest person on earth and that someone should tell it straight to his face.

"I know the man. I'll see what I can do," said the friend.

A few weeks later the two ladies met each other again.

"What did you do?" asked the woman who had complained about the pharmacist. "I went to the pharmacy again and the man was completely changed. He was nice and kind. Did you confront him about his behavior?"

"Well, not really," said the friend. "I told him that you think he is a charming man."

We once had the opportunity to conduct a workshop at the Bechterew Psycho-Neurological Institute in Leningrad. During the workshop we demonstrated our approach by interviewing clients presently in treatment at the hospital. Valentine, a psychiatrist from the neurosis department, had brought a young man named Anatoli to the workshop for consultation. Valentine, Anatoli, and our translator were sitting with us in front of an audience of some hundred professionals.

Holding Anatoli's records in his hands, Valentine started the session by beginning to describe Anatoli's case to the audience. Tapani politely interrupted him, "Excuse me, Valentine," he said, "would you mind if we started by asking a few questions?"

"Not at all," said Valentine and signaled us to go ahead.

"First of all, we are curious about whether there are other people present besides Valentine who are acquainted with Anatoli?" asked Ben.

There were two psychologists in the audience who knew Anatoli. We asked them to join us in the front and they did so.

We then continued by collecting some basic information. We learned that Anatoli had come to the hospital for treatment from a distant town in the north of Russia and that he had been on the waiting list to enter the highly respected neurosis department of the hospital for almost two years. He had now been under treatment for one month and during this time he had been almost out of touch with his family, having talked to his wife only once by telephone. We asked Anatoli what he thought about his treatment and discovered that there was a warm and confidential relationship between him and Dr. Valentine.

"Has Anatoli already made progress?" asked Ben. The answer was a definite yes. We used the blackboard to gather a list of indications of progress.

Still without any information about Anatoli's problem, we invited people to take a look into the future.

"Do your patients sometimes send you postcards, say at Christmas or New Year, after they have left the hospital?" asked Tapani.

"Yes, it happens very often," said Valentine.

"And do you ever get postcards with good news, postcards where people write that they are grateful for the treatment they received and that things are fine?"

Again the answer was in the affirmative. We then turned to Anatoli and asked him if he could imagine that he would one day send such a postcard from his home town to the staff of the department. He readily agreed.

"Let's suppose that Anatoli will one day write a postcard to the staff. What kind of a picture do you imagine he would choose?"

"A picture of Misha," said one of the two psychologists.

"What is a Misha?" asked Ben, revealing his ignorance. It was explained that Misha is a teddy bear, the cute one that was the emblem for the Olympic Games in Moscow.

Anatoli gladly approved. Ben drew a picture of a teddy bear inside a rectangle and asked the audience to tell him what Misha symbolizes. We were told that Misha is a symbol which combines strength and kindness.

"Perhaps Misha symbolizes the qualities Anatoli was able to find within himself as a result of the treatment," said Ben and asked, "What would you write on the back of the card? Would you perhaps start with a word of thanks?"

"Certainly," said Anatoli.

"And who would you thank in particular?"

"I would thank all the staff and particularly Dr. Valentine," said Anatoli.

"What else would you write? Probably you would want to write something about how things are going with you."

Anatoli said that he would write that he no longer has the problems he used to have and that he is happy with his wife and two sons. We asked him if he would write about any other major changes in his life and he said no. We then raised the question of what had made this change possible and took suggestions from the audience. These included:

• The treatment, and particularly the relationship with Dr. Valentine, had helped Anatoli to regain his dignity as a person.

• Anatoli had realized how much his family actually meant to him.

• Anatoli had discovered the Misha-bear within him.

• Anatoli had understood that there is a time to talk about problems and that there is also a time to refrain from talking about them.

This last suggestion, which we presented ourselves, was based on the idea that sometimes problems are maintained simply by the fact that people think and talk about them excessively. It was this suggestion that Anatoli chose to be put on his postcard.

Finally, we recommended that sometime during the following week Valentine call together a meeting with Anatoli and anyone else concerned, such as the psychologist who had joined us on the scene. In this meeting a letter was to be written to Anatoli's wife. In the letter the wife should be informed about Anatoli's progress and about how she, the children, and also Anatoli's parents, who lived in the same household, had each in unique ways contributed to Anatoli's recovery. Our recommendation was approved of and we ended the session.

After Anatoli had left we continued for a while to discuss the session. One psychiatrist stood up and said he was doubtful about the usefulness of this type of approach in this kind of a case. He explained that Anatoli was an Afghanistan War veteran who, according to him, suffered from post-traumatic stress disorder. Valentine, Anatoli's doctor, then explained that he had, indeed, initially considered the possibility of post-traumatic disorder, but that since Anatoli himself had disagreed with this conceptualization he had decided to drop it.

The discussion gave us an opportunity to present our own view of the significance of untoward life experiences. We explained that, rather than seeing such events as the source of problems, we like to think of them as learning opportunities that can help people become "strong and kind"—just like the Misha-bear.

Through our translator we were later informed that Anatoli had, indeed, recovered from his problems. Furthermore, he had been granted release of his "dispansersatsia," that is, from his obligation to report at regular intervals to his local psychiatric clinic.

Traditionally psychotherapy has revolved around identifying and trying to understand the causes of people's problems. Such an approach has been directed towards defining additional problems that are believed to be responsible for causing the complaint, the symptom, or the presenting problem. For example, if a person suffers from nightmares, according to this approach the therapist would explore presumed underlying psychological or interpersonal causes for those nightmares. Thus, the interview would focus on the individual's present and past difficulties. In all likelihood problems would be discovered and then these would be viewed as the cause of the nightmares. Finally, a plan would be devised with the aim of curing the underlying problem rather than dealing directly with the presenting problem.

In many situations this approach is quite appropriate. For example, when a machine breaks or someone has a fever, discovering the cause of the problem is important, as it tells us what to do. However, when it comes to complex human problems – psychological difficulties, interpersonal conflicts or even wide-scale social questions – this approach becomes problematic. Human problems are so complex that it is only natural that in attempting to understand the causes of problems people end up with differing explanations. As different explanations call for different courses of action, collaboration becomes difficult. People may even fall out with one another when they experience each other's explanations as unjustified accusations and become compelled to defend their own explanations.

For example, a pupil is misbehaving at school. His teacher is likely to think that the misbehavior is caused by some underlying problem present within the child, such as a short attention span, lack of motivation, or disrespect for the teacher. Whatever the teacher thinks the underlying problem to be, he or she is likely to believe that it, in turn, is the result of some further disturbance, possibly inadequate parental guidance or conflicts within the family. The parents of the pupil are tempted, in their turn, to think that their child's misbehavior is a result of the teacher's inability to understand their child. The pupil himself may put blame on the school in general. Finally, the parties may learn about each other's explanations, and then feel unjustifiably accused. An end result may well be unintentional reciprocal blaming, which makes solving the problem an unlikely prospect.

In our search for alternative ways of talking about problems we have been drawn to the traditions of family and brief therapy. Over the years we have gradually found a number of useful ideas for conducting therapeutic conversations and consultations which we will refer to in this book as "solution talk." This way of working is characterized both by an atmosphere of openness and by what could be characterized as a constructive way of talking. This conversational style is achieved by thinking positively and by focusing on subjects that foster hope, such as resources, progress, and the future.

For the purposes of teaching we have distinguished a number of aspects that we feel characterize solution talk. Each chapter in the book highlights a particular aspect of solution talk.

We open with the chapter "The Fall of the Wall," in which we familiarize the reader with the evolution of our way of working with people. We describe our journey from brief therapy supervision using a one-way mirror to our current model of working where clients and eventually family members, friends, other helpers or trainees all sit together in the same room discussing problems – or rather solutions – in an encouraging and predominantly forward-looking atmosphere.

In the second chapter, "The Role of the Past," we discuss the role of history in therapy and suggest that, rather than seeing the past as a source of people's problems, it may be viewed as a resource which can be of help in solving problems. We also present ways of dealing with past-related issues involving guilt, bitterness, or grief.

In chapter three, "Making and Unmaking Connections," we face the fact that in many cases several simultaneous problems exist. We suggest that the problems be seen as independent rather than interconnected and that they be viewed in a way where one problem can help in the solution of another.

In the fourth chapter, "Watchful Wording," we take a critical look at conventional psychiatric and psychological terminology. We propose that many widely used psychological concepts and diagnostic terms can be replaced by more creative or favorable words and expressions.

In chapter five, "Fruitful Explanations," we propose that in order to carry out constructive conversations it is not necessary to forego explanation. However, we suggest that instead of using conventional explanations which often involve ideas of deficiency or dysfunction, therapists favor inventive or even absurd explanations.

In chapter six, "Future Visions," we demonstrate the usefulness of inviting people to generate visions of a positive future and present various ways of engaging clients in this process.

Chapter seven, entitled "Building on Progress," highlights what we see as the central theme of solution talk. With the help of case examples we show that even at times when progress is meager, focusing on progress can establish a positive and productive tone for the conversation.

In chapter eight, "Sharing Credit," we discuss the importance of thanking people for their contribution to any progress, a theme that distinguishes our work. We argue that sharing credit is a way of increasing collaboration and encouraging progress.

In chapter nine, "Problems as Friends," we propose that people be helped to see their problems in a positive light, as allies or as teachers rather than enemies or nuisances. We maintain that holding a positive view of problems helps one to deal with them.

In the final chapter, "Teaching and Training," we describe how the ideas and principles of solution talk can be taught to other people in a manner consistent with those ideas and principles.

Throughout the text we have provided case examples. Many of the examples are drawn from our training seminars or workshops, but some date back to the time before our collaboration and some are drawn from our private practice.

We have chosen to report our case examples in the style of storytelling, with the intention of conveying the spirit of our way of working. The dialogues presented are not word-for-word transcripts of the interviews but edited versions of conversations that took place. As is customary in therapeutic literature, all names and other details which could lead to the identification of clients have been changed.

In many of the examples presented in this book the consultation appears to have been helpful to clients. This may give the false impression that we always succeed in bringing about positive results. In order to guard against any misunderstanding, it should be said that over the years we have also worked with a number of cases where goals have not been reached. Furthermore, even if we like to think that in the presented cases our involvement has been a contribution, we are fully aware that in reality there are many other encounters and occurrences in our clients' lives that could equally well be held responsible for their improvement.

Finally, we want to emphasize that the list of various aspects of solution talk is not intended to be exhaustive; it is a selection of preferred themes and principles we have found useful in guiding conversations with people so as to encourage collaboration, optimism, and creativity in people.

Solution Talk

Hosting Therapeutic Conversations

1

THE FALL OF THE WALL

When we started to teach methods of brief therapy to professionals in the mid-eighties we adopted the trainer-centered live supervision model commonly used in family and brief therapy training programs worldwide. This model involves the use of two rooms: a therapy room where the therapist-trainee interviews his or her clients, and an observation room where the supervisor and the other trainees observe the session through a one-way screen or, as in our case, a closed circuit TV. There is an intercom telephone between the two rooms so that the supervisor can call the therapist and give him or her instructions about how to conduct the interview.

Our first training group consisted of some 20 professionals, a group that convened for one full day a week. The trainees brought, one after the other, a client from their respective working places to the center for a consultation or a live supervised therapy session. As a rule there were two clients per day, one in the morning and another in the afternoon. Any remaining time was used for discussing cases and issues raised by the trainees.

We used to begin the consultations with a presession discussion during which the therapist told about the client to the group. We discussed the case in terms of what was "really" going on in the case and made suggestions to the therapist concerning questions to be asked in the session.

When the clients arrived they were escorted by the therapist to the therapy room. The rest of the group remained with us in the adjacent room where we observed the interview through

1

the monitor. Over the course of the session we used to call therapists frequently on the intercom phone and give them instructions about what to say. Sometimes we ended up communicating with the client through the therapist. We would tell the therapist to forward a message to the client, who would then respond to our message, provoking us to send another message and so on, with the result that the poor therapist was sometimes reduced to a mouthpiece. When we felt that the therapist did not see what we intended to tell him or her through the intercom, we knocked on the door of the therapy room and called the therapist out for a brief "brainwash."

Towards the end of the session we usually took a break, during which the clients were asked to go out for a cup of coffee while the therapist joined the group to plan an intervention. This usually involved a new view of what the problem was all about, also called reframing, coupled with a suggestion for a relevant home assignment. When the clients returned the therapist delivered the intervention and closed the session.

The following case is drawn from our very first training seminar. Here the therapist, who was a psychiatrist at a mental hospital, was instructed to recommend to the clients a metaphorical task, a procedure originally described by Milton Erickson (Boyd, 1987). The story is told by Tapani who was the primary supervisor in the session.

The Time of Ice Breakup

The therapist brought in a couple. The wife had recently been hospitalized because of a severe depression. She had rapidly improved and at the time of the consultation discharge was already being talked about. Plans had been made that after discharge she would continue therapy with the therapist on an outpatient basis. I instructed the therapist through the intercom to focus on questions related to the spouses relationship with one another as well as with their in-laws. During the interview it emerged among other things that, despite the fact that the couple had been married for several years, the issue of having a child had not been addressed. When asked about this, both partners appeared keen on having a child in the future but explained that she had to be healthy before this was possible.

The couple's situation brought to me an image of a river in spring just before the ice breaks up. During the intermission I suggested to the therapist that the couple's problem could be seen in terms of preparing for ice break-up. I asked him if he had ever seen a river when the ice breaks up and the big white chunks of ice float down the stream. The therapist said that he had lived most of his childhood years close to a river and knew exactly what I was talking about. I said that, instead of simply sharing this metaphor with the couple, we might ask them to go together and find a place near a river where they could, when the time was due, observe the magnificent sight of ice breakup. One of the trainees added that the husband should be given the instructions to take his wife to various sites near the river in order to let her choose the actual place where they would then witness the ice breakup. The therapist accepted these suggestions without hesitation and delivered the recommendation graciously to the couple. We later heard from him that the couple had, indeed, carried out the task and that the wife had gradually overcome her depression.

Even if our trainees usually complied with our ideas and suggestions, there were times when they appeared reluctant to follow our advice. At first we thought this was simply because the kind of therapy we exercised, unconventional as it was, appeared so alien to them. As we discussed the issue with the trainees, we gradually realized that when trainees did not accept our suggestions, it was not so much because they were being conventional, but because their idea about the underlying cause of the problem was at odds with ours.

We therefore started to invite trainees to share their assumptions about the causes of clients' problems during intervention planning breaks. Without criticizing any of their explanations, we simply recorded them all on the flip chart. This procedure served as a way of demonstrating that there were always multiple plausible explanations to account for a given problem.

This exploration of different explanations turned out to be an exciting and entertaining procedure. We did not stop at what our trainees first said but continued by asking repeated "why" questions, not unlike small children, until the explanations began to border on the absurd. The following dialogue serves as an example.

"Why is he behaving like this?"
"He is too tied up to his parents."
"Why?"
"Because his mother does not want to let go of him."
"Why?"
"Because she needs him for her own purposes."
"Why?"
"Because the marriage does not satisfy her."
"Why?"
"Because the husband is so distant."
"Why?"
"Because he is unable to be close to his wife."
"Why?"
"Because he is so tied up to his mother . . . "

Discussions about explanations were used for the purpose of questioning conventional ways of explaining human problems and increasing the trainees' ability to think of alternative explanations devoid of allegations of fault.

These "explanation analyses" were initially carried out in clients' absence. One day a trainee observed that if she were the client she would like to be allowed to listen to the group's conversation about explanations. Since this seemed like a good idea, we decided to invite our clients to join us. We soon found that clients were not only interested in listening to our dialogue but also keen on taking part in it. They seemed particularly to enjoy situations when ideas indicative of underlying pathology became transformed from excruciating truths to nothing more than points of view.

Disclosing diverse points of views to clients soon became an integral part of our work. We did it regularly not only with the clients who came to the center for consultation but also with clients whose problems were discussed in the group in their absence. When therapists wanted to discuss a case without bringing the client in for a consultation, we often recorded our conversation on a video and sent the cassette through the therapist to the client. A few times, when we interviewed a family where one member was presently in institutional care, we recorded the conversation on video and gave the cassette to the family to take to the institution for the staff to see.

The practice of exposing different explanations to clients paved the way for the next step on our path towards increased openness: We decided to abandon the twin room system and to invite clients and the therapist to sit in the same room with the whole group throughout the session. We also gave up the custom of letting the therapist present the case to the group in advance, instead asking the therapist and the client to introduce the problem together at the beginning of the session.

The following example is about a middle-aged house wife invited to the group by her gynecologist, who was in training with us. We collaborated in conducting the interview.

The Therapeutic Secret

Lilian had one day begun to cry in the appointment room. When the doctor had asked her what was the matter, she explained that her husband was extremely jealous, so much so that in his rage he had physically attacked her a number of times. Lilian had said that her husband continuously suspected that there was another man and that it was impossible for her to convince him otherwise. Whenever she had tried he had become even more angry and had accused her of lying. The problem had lasted for several years, gradually becoming worse. The doctor had met with Lilian twice just to discuss this problem. Since there was no progress, she had decided to ask Lilian to come for a consultation session with us.

After we had found out all of the above we began our inquiry about explanations.

"Lilian, does your husband know you are here?" asked Tapani.

"Heavens no. I could never tell him. You see, I cannot talk with him about this. If I try it only makes it worse," said Lilian.

"OK, but suppose he was here and we would ask him, what do you think he would say is the cause of this problem?"

"He would say I'm lying. No doubt about it."

"And you? What is your explanation?"

"I think it must be some sort of an illness."

"I see, and what about your doctor? What do you think she thinks is the cause?"

"I think she agrees that it is a mental disturbance," Lilian said. The doctor nodded in agreement.

"So what you are saying is that your husband needs treatment. Could you ask him to come with you somewhere to talk about it?"

"No way. It's impossible."

"What if the doctor called your husband and asked him to come with you for a session. Would that be possible?"

"No. That would be even worse. He would find out that I have been talking about this and all hell would break loose," Lilian said. She appeared to know what she was talking about. The doctor added, "He needs treatment, but there is no way of making him understand it."

"All right. So there is the explanation that this would be an illness," said Tapani and explained, "We have also thought much about jealousy and tried to make sense of it. We have found, for example, that frequently when a person begins to suspect his or her partner of infidelity without a reason there actually exists someone else – not a sexual partner as the jealous person thinks, but a person such as a mother, friend, child, or even a therapist with whom the suspected person talks confidentially about things so that the jealous person feels left out and put in second place." As Tapani finished describing this theory of ours, Lilian became reflective and said that she has, indeed, a friend like that with whom she shares everything, also her husband's jealousy.

Ben then introduces still another alternative explanation to account for unfounded jealousy. According to this view it is a result of a vicious circle; the jealous person realizes that his behavior is defined as sick by the other and becomes offended. As a result of the insult, he becomes furious and increases his efforts to find proof of infidelity, which is his only way of contesting the accusation that he is sick. In this vicious circle both parties have a good reason to feel offended – the suspected person for being unjustly accused of infidelity and the suspecting person for being unjustly accused of being mentally ill. Both of our alternative theories seemed to make sense to Lilian and the doctor.

We then announced that on the basis of these theories we had an idea of what Lilian might do to help her husband overcome his jealousy. We also warned her that our suggestion was likely to be quite different from anything that had been suggested so far. As she and the doctor responded with curiosity, we went on to give her the following advice, "You should think of a secret that you could tell to your husband but no-one else, not even your best friend or your doctor. There is no rush for you to think of it now, because it is important that it be something significant. It is also utterly important that, before you agree to tell it to him, you make absolutely sure that he will promise not tell it to anyone. Only after he has given you his word are you to reveal the big secret to him." Lilian understood the rationale of the task and agreed to do it.

We heard about Lilian some half a year later. She had completed the task and found it useful. The following summer had been like a new honeymoon and there had been no more attacks of jealousy. When the doctor had asked Lilian about the secret she had refused to say what it was.

Our experiences with the joint conversations were so rewarding that the format soon became the standard. We have since found that this arrangement has many advantages. It allows us as supervisors to better influence the course of the conversation and makes it possible for us to communicate simultaneously with both the client and the therapist. The atmosphere in the room is usually pleasant and the conversation lively. With our own example we encourage participants to be as informal as possible. Coffee is usually available during the meeting, people address each other by first names, and laughter is frequently heard.

The joint conversation training format has also been well received by the clients. Contrary to the common presupposition that most people would rather not talk about their problems within a large group, we have found that they often approve of it. Moreover, clients often seem to find it exciting to be surrounded by many professionals all discussing their problem in a respectful manner. We have made a habit of asking clients at the end of sessions to say something about how they experienced the meeting. As a rule people respond by saying that the experience was pleasant. Some people point out that they were nervous at first when joining the group but that they began to feel increasingly comfortable as the conversation unfolded.

From People with Problems to a Problem with People

Over the years the concept of client has acquired an ever broader meaning in our work. Whereas the word was originally used to refer to individuals, couples, or families seeking help for a problem it now stands for any person or group of people with a common concern. We have had as clients in our sessions parents seeking advice in dealing with their offspring, groups of peers concerned about a common friend, professional staff groups with internal conflicts, managers with organizational problems, and teachers with school problems. Not uncommonly our trainees have invited their friends or acquaintances in for a consultation.

In the early phases of our work we used to try to convince the therapist to get as many family members as possible to join the consultation session. Gradually, we have given up this practice and now simply advise clients to decide for themselves who they wish to invite along. Consequently, we have had in our sessions boyfriends and girlfriends, schoolmates, teachers, counselors, social welfare workers, health visitors, staff from residential institutions, general practitioners, community volunteers, members of church congregations, etc.

The following example involves vicarious work with a school class. We dealt with the problem through the school counselor without having direct contact with the teacher or the pupils.

The Terrible Threesome

Mervi was a school psychologist in training with us. She told us that she had been asked for advice by a young female teacher who was in trouble with a special class consisting of four 13-year-old boys. The boys had been removed from their own classes because of chronic disruptive behavior. Despite the fact that she had no training in special education, the teacher had been put in charge of teaching the group. Her problem was that the boys were totally out of control. Mervi had visited the class two times and confirmed that when the boys chose to be present they disobeyed all orders of the teacher and concentrated on making trouble.

Mervi had been thinking about inviting the teacher and the boys to the center for consultation. We suggested that before doing that she go into the classroom and inform the teacher and the boys that she had presented the problem at our training course. She was to add that the training group, which consisted of doctors, psychologists, and other professionals, had become very interested in the problem. The group now wanted to have a clearer picture of what was actually going on in the class during lessons, in order to be able to think of something that could be done to solve the problem. With this introduction Mervi was to ask the boys to behave exactly the way they usually did in order for her to be able to record one or two lessons on video.

Mervi carried out the suggestion. She produced as much as three hours of videotape and edited it down to 20 minutes of agonizing scenes of outrageous classroom behavior. After reviewing the whole tape, the training group was divided into small groups that were given the task of developing a suggestion for Mervi to bring to the teacher. We took notes of all the suggestions on the flip chart.

One of the groups suggested that the parents of these boys should be invited to the school to see the video and to discuss what could be done to solve the problem. Another group suggested that the teacher should allow the boys to watch the video and ask them to come up with a solution. Still another group suggested that Mervi should ask the teacher and the boys to make another video where the boys would behave in a most proper fashion. Then the two videos would be shown as teaching videos with royalties paid to the boys. Finally, we handed to Mervi all the flip chart sheets and asked her to show them to the teacher and the boys.

The next week Mervi reported that she had carried out the instruction and that each of our suggestions had raised a lively discussion in the classroom. Follow-up several months later revealed that the boys had improved their behavior significantly and the teacher was no longer distressed. This had happened even though none of our ingenious suggestions were ever carried out. Perhaps the project had helped to bring the teacher and the boys together. Another possibility is that the boys began to behave out of the fear that the video would actually be shown to their parents.

We have found that the word "client" is not always an appropriate term to refer to those people who come to discuss a given concern with us. For example, if Juhani's parents come to consult with us about Juhani's behavior, then who is our client? Juhani, his parents, or all of them? If Juhani's girlfriend Olivia comes along with the parents to the meeting, should she also be regarded as a client? What about the social worker who has been talking with Juhani but was unable to come to the meeting even though he intended to?

In one of our meetings, when the session was over, our clients, a couple along with their therapist, did not make a move to leave, even though all the usual closing questions, such as "What did you think about the session?" and "Would you care to let us know after a couple of months how things are going?" had been posed. Tapani asked if they had heard the story of the man whose wife's guests stayed at the house beyond his bedtime. He was a polite man who did not want to offend his wife's guests in any way by rushing them so he came downstairs and asked his wife, in passing, "I wonder what time the guests would be at home if they left now?" Tapani then looked at our guests and said, "And what time you would be at home if you left now?" Everyone burst out laughing and our guests said, smilingly, that they got the message. Since the incident we have, for lack of a better word, sometimes used the word "guests" to denote those people, inclusive of eventual professionals involved with the case, who come to a meeting to discuss a problem.

Open Cards

The joint discussion format reflects the conviction that it is not necessary for therapists to strategize behind the client's back or to carry out conversations that are not meant to reach the ears of the client. This is not to say that the therapist should not be directive. In fact, as we see it, the role of the therapist or the conductor of the session is similar to that of a chairman of any meeting or—in a sense—a talk-show host. The therapist controls the course of the session, raises and drops issues, and influences the mood of the session through his or her own behavior.

Since there are no predetermined rules of procedure for joint discussions, it becomes possible to engage clients in decisions concerning the agenda for the session. For example, we once had as a client a father with his six-year-old daughter who had the problem of soiling her pants. The girl's mother had died when she was four and since then, wherever the father had taken his daughter for help, professionals had bombarded both of them with endless questions about the mother's death and the girl's emotional reactions to this loss. At the very beginning of our session we asked the father whether he wanted us to discuss the question of what was causing the problem or whether he preferred that we just offer him suggestions for solving it. He said he had had enough explanations and was more than ready for practical advice. We accepted his request and focused in the session on offering him several practical ideas about how to deal with the problem.

The following example illustrates the involvement of the client in the negotiation of the agenda for the meeting.

Multiple Choice

We once had an opportunity to present our way of working to a group of family therapy students at a training institute in the United States. During the day we interviewed several clients, one of whom was a young man who suffered from a common problem, fear of social situations.

We began the session by offering an outline of the various approaches that we would commonly use in such cases. Each approach was briefly described and recorded on the blackboard. The choices included: (1) challenging preexisting explanations and finding new explanations to replace the old ones; (2) generating creative solutions without bothering about explanations at all; (3) focusing on whatever progress had already taken place and encouraging the changes that were already underway; (4) approaching the problem indirectly by creating a metaphor of the problem and then finding a solution for the metaphor. After all the choices had been presented, the client took a few minutes to decide. He chose the second alternative which then became the approach for the remaining three-quarters of the session.

The agenda can always be renegotiated during the session if there are signs that the client (or anyone else present) is not satisfied with the way things are being discussed. We have found that what is sometimes referred to as "resistance" in psychotherapy literature can be more aptly defined as "discontent regarding the agenda." When clients appear "resistant," this can be seen as a sign of their wish to renegotiate the agenda for the meeting. The following vignette is drawn from a session Ben conducted with a couple who had been invited for a consultation by an alcohol counselor.

The Question of Agenda

While we were discussing the husband's drinking behavior and engaging in fantasies of what things would look like were he to stop drinking, the wife grew increasingly impatient. I noticed that some of the therapists who were sitting in the session grew equally impatient with the wife. I suspected, and later confirmed, that they saw her as "resistant" and as not even wanting him, deep down, to stop drinking.

We took a brief break during which we discussed the wife's response and looked for a positive way of understanding her behavior. We rejoined the couple, and, addressing the wife, I said, "I have the feeling that we are not on the right track in this conversation. Is there something I have failed to take into account?" She explained that even if his drinking was, no doubt, a problem, a much more pressing issue for both of them was the behavior of their teenage daughter. The wife described the daughter's problems and started crying as she expressed how bewildered she was about how to help her. We decided to set aside, for the time being, the husband's drinking problem and had a constructive conversation with the couple about how they could deal with the daughter.

Audience Participation

Joint discussions allow everyone present to become participants in the ongoing conversation. We encourage everyone to
ask questions and share their ideas. Towards the end of the
session we often divide the group into smaller groups, each of
which presents to the clients a recommendation about what to
do to solve the problem. We have found that as a rule clients
prefer sessions with active group participation.

We have sometimes invited participants to share personal
experiences they believe might be useful to the client. The first
time we experimented with this was when we interviewed a
teenage girl who had come for a consultation because of anxiety and trembling of hands in the company of unfamiliar people. Tapani asked the group if others present had suffered from
the same problem at some point in their lives. Several people
raised their hands. He then asked the girl if she would be interested in hearing some of these stories. Since the girl was keen,
many of us shared our personal experiences. We were later informed by the girl's therapist that upon leaving the building
she had said, "I would never have imagined that so many of
those therapists have had the same problem as I have."

The following example is a synopsis of a joint session, which
took place in a workshop Ben conducted in Sweden. In the
session participants spontaneously wished to share their personal feelings and experiences with the clients.

The Courageous Family

A child psychiatrist who had been working with a 17-
year-old girl, Maria, and her family invited the whole family to a session with the group. Present in the session were
mother and her current live-in boyfriend; Lena, the younger daughter, who was 12; and Maria, accompanied by her
boyfriend. Maria sat silently for the first half of session,
with her face down and covered by her hair; however, she
gradually opened up and became an active participant in
the discussion.

I began the session by making contact with each member of the family and asking questions about how they had experienced the treatment so far and what their goals were for the future. The discussion soon began to focus on what had happened in the near past. We learned that father had committed suicide in a dreadful way; he had killed himself in front of his family.

Immediately following father's death Maria had become withdrawn and had begun to talk about joining father in the other world. By the time of the session she had attempted suicide four times. In spite of this, the family had forged its way through the tragedy. Both mother and Maria had found themselves boyfriends who had been of enormous support to them. Maria's boyfriend was not exactly what mother had hoped for; however, given the circumstances, she was quite happy that Maria had something to think about other than her dead father. Lena, Maria's sister, seemed to have adjusted reasonably well to her father's death, even though she couldn't remember much of the tragic night. Mother and Maria spoke openly about the incident, revealing details of what had actually happened. We also discussed many things that had happened in the family after father's suicide and the various ways in which family members, including Maria's boyfriend, had helped one another to survive.

The story was so tragic and the family members appeared so courageous amidst their burden that the feeling of respect towards the family was almost palpable in the room. I suggested that, since their sharing of their story had undoubtedly had an intense effect on each of us, we might share our feelings and thoughts with them. We all spoke, each in a personal way, about our admiration for them, about recollections of tragic events in our own lives, and about what the session with them had brought to us both personally and professionally. When everyone had spoken, the family members, including Maria, thanked us earnestly. Mother pointed out that the session had also been a worthwhile experience for them.

Months later I heard from the organizers of the workshop that Maria was making steady progress and that the child psychiatrist in charge of the case felt that the session had a positive impact on the family.

The following is yet another example of letting participants take an active role in the conversation. The example is drawn from a workshop where there were over 60 participants present with chairs placed in a large circle.

Role Reversal

In a one-day workshop we gave in the United States we presented before noon an outline of our ideas on solution talk. During the lunch break one of the participants came to us and asked us if we would be willing to demonstrate our approach live. She said she had been seeing a couple who might be willing to come in for a session the same afternoon. We encouraged her to go ahead and invite the couple. She phoned them up and they agreed to come.

The therapist had met with the couple, who were both in their fifties, a half a dozen times, and during the introduction we got the impression that the therapy had been helpful.

We suggested that instead of asking questions about their problems we might organize the interview in a different way. We explained to the spouses that this was a workshop on how to solve human problems in a constructive way and asked them if they were curious to know more about what we had been discussing in the group up until now. Since the spouses expressed their interest we suggested that the participants tell them what issues had been talked about before noon. We encouraged the participants to do this personally, by talking about the application of these principles in their own lives and relationships rather than with their clients. We invited the couple to comment on each of the reports.

One by one the participants began to speak about what had been meaningful to them during the morning. Several persons related personal experiences from their own lives to illustrate the point they were making. For example, one person spoke about the importance of focusing on progress rather than problems and told a story about how he had used this method to overcome a long-term problem with his wife. Another person spoke about the usefulness of sharing future fantasies and told how she had used this approach with her son.

The clients responded to each of the participants. Occasionally they said that a particular point was not applicable to their situation but most of the time they agreed with what the participants said. We didn't learn much about the couple's problems; instead, they learned a great deal about us. At the end of the session we asked the spouses to share their feelings about the session. They said that not only had they enjoyed it, but that the discussion had confirmed to them that they had approached their problem in the right way and that their therapist had done an excellent job with them.

Our decision to sit together with our clients and trainees has required us to change our habitual ways of talking about people and their problems. It has compelled us to look for respectful ways of conversing which, despite the number of people present, allow clients to enjoy the sessions and feel dignified when they leave. The guidelines that we have identified will be discussed in the following chapters.

2

THE ROLE OF THE PAST

It's never too late to have a happy childhood.

For decades the dominant notion within psychiatry and psychotherapy has been that the causes of psychological problems have their origins in the past. It has become commonplace to think that untoward childhood experiences and also later stressful events leave their mark on people and show up as symptoms in later life. This belief is now encountered not only in psychiatric and psychological textbooks but also in the media and in daily clinical practice. For instance, one day we received a phone call from a school nurse. She wanted to refer to us a 10-year-old boy who refused to go to school. Among the first things she explained was that the boy's father had died of cancer. Later on during the conversation it emerged that the boy's father had died of cancer six years ago, while the problems had started only in the last year. Yet the implicit assumption was that the father's death was somehow responsible for the boy's refusal to attend school.

Our history is an integral part of ourselves. As long as we think of the past as the source of our problems, we set up, in a sense, an adversarial relationship within ourselves. The past, very humanly, responds negatively to criticism and blaming but favorably to respect and stroking. The past prefers to be seen as a resource, a store of memories, good and bad, and a source of wisdom emanating from life experience.

The following example dates back to the time Ben was doing his residency at the university psychiatric hospital. It illustrates the all too common situation where a person thinks of his parents as the source of his misery.

Black and Blue

A young man in his early twenties, Esko, was admitted to the ward because of acute confusion. Esko had recently moved to Helsinki from the north of Finland in order to study at the technological university. He did not have many friends and used to travel a great distance every weekend to visit his parents. Some years previously he had suffered a brief psychotic episode, during which he had been hospitalized. Since that time he had been on medication.

Esko's looks confirmed his confused state. His longish hair was a mess and his eyes seemed much too big for their sockets. He walked nervously about inside and outside the hospital. When he spoke he always came up with new plans for the future. When I told him that I would like to arrange a meeting with him and his parents, he was taken by surprise and objected, arguing that it would turn into a disaster because he only fought with them. I had learned, from reading the books of Jay Haley, that it is the task of the family therapist to make sure that parents and children do not argue during therapy. I said to Esko, "Don't worry, I will not allow you to argue with your parents. If you insist on arguing, you will have to leave the room." Esko accepted this and agreed to invite his parents to a meeting at the hospital.

When the parents arrived, they said that this was the first time they had ever been invited to talk with anybody responsible for Esko's treatment. They had never spoken with his individual therapist whom he had visited regularly twice a week for some years. Neither had they been invited to the hospital during his first psychotic breakdown.

We began the session by talking about history. I learned that Esko had been an exceptionally intelligent boy. He had always done well at school, but at the age of 18 he had suddenly become confused and been taken to a psychiatric hospital. Since then he had attended individual psychotherapy twice and sometimes three times a week. Gradually Esko had adopted the habit of blaming his parents for his problems. Whenever he was at home he accused either his mother, his father or both of having done this or that wrong to him in the past. Esko's parents replied to his constant criticism with futile attempts at defense. The more they defended themselves the more Esko attacked them.

I said to the parents that there was no positive value in Esko's blaming them for his problems. I explained that as long as Esko kept blaming them he would not take responsibility for initiating measures to solve his own problems. Esko sat quietly and listened attentively. I then suggested to the parents that they could help Esko to put an end to his blaming them.

"That's easier said than done," said father, "What can we do? We've tried everything."

"It might be useful if you stopped replying to his accusations. You should not bother to defend yourselves."

Both parents seemed to think that this was a sensible idea. I then asked Esko to start criticizing his parents so that we could see if they would be able to carry out the task. Esko was taken aback and quite unable to accuse his parents when told to do so. To give the parents a chance to practice, I took Esko's role and criticized the parents. "You have caused my problems because you never cared for me!" I accused.

It became evident that the parents, no matter how hard they tried, were unable to abstain from defending themselves against criticism. They just couldn't help it. I even asked them to supervise each other, but this led to arguments between them about whether their responses counted as defensive or not.

When we were about to end the session, I said that it was so important for Esko to stop blaming his parents that I would like them to practice abstaining from defending themselves. I suggested that each time either one of the parents caught the other in the act of defending, he or she should immediately, without saying a word, signal the fact by pinching the defender in the rear. In a friendly manner I tapped Esko on the shoulder and said, "I want you to give them a really hard time so that they get lots of practice. Next time we meet, I will be personally inspecting their behinds and I want to see them black and blue!" All three members of the family left the session laughing.

Esko visited his parents the following weekend. When he returned to the hospital he enthusiastically reported that there had been no arguments at all between him and his parents on this visit. When I saw the family a month later at the time of discharge, Esko's parents confirmed that he had not only made a lot of progress but that he had actually stopped criticizing them altogether. Several months later we received a postcard from Esko in which he informed us that he was now doing fine and had just passed the entrance examination to change to study in the college he had always desired.

The belief that tragedies of the past cause later problems and render people vulnerable to future strain can become a self-fulfilling prophecy. Conversely, to think of one's past as a resource may help people in achieving their goals. Peggy Penn, family therapist at the Ackerman Institute in New York, once said that she sometimes asks people whether they think the hardships they have suffered have made them stronger or weaker. Invariably, according to her, people answer that their hardships have made them stronger.

The following example dates back to the time Ben was doing his residency in a psychiatric hospital. The young man in this case was helped to pull himself out of a difficult situation by the conviction that his tragic past had made him stronger rather than weaker.

Discharge Without Mercy

Hessu was an 18-year-old who had been hospitalized for having slashed his wrists after a bout of heavy drinking. His history was a tragedy with many difficulties and dis-

appointments. Due to his parents' severe alcohol problems, he had been taken into custody at an early age by
child welfare workers; they placed him, together with his
younger brother, in a children's home. There had been
gross difficulties on his way to adulthood, but recently, as
he approached the coming of age, he had begun to study
to make up for his missed school classes. He had finally
become interested in getting his school-leaving certificate,
which is essential for entering any vocational school.

On the ward Hessu appeared to be a determined young
man who really did intend to regain control of his life. The
special teacher at the hospital reported that he had
started to help Hessu with his studies. Hessu was now
doing his chores and getting support from his girlfriend
who was studying with him. Contact was established with
Hessu's social worker at the department of child welfare
and plans were made about where Hessu should live after
his hospital treatment was over.

All seemed to be going well when one evening, after
having been in the hospital only three weeks, Hessu came
back heavily drunk from one of his evening leaves. There
were strict regulations on the ward against the use of
alcohol; intoxication during treatment meant discontinu-
ation of treatment and discharge from the hospital. Since
I was in charge of Hessu's treatment I announced to the
staff on the round that he would have to be discharged. I
then personally informed Hessu about the decision. With
a look of appeal on his face he asked to be allowed to stay,
but I held onto my judgment, which I thought was fair. I
explained to Hessu, "You know that we all like you and we
would be happy to keep you here. However, if I do not
discharge you, that would mean that I think you are
weak, that you wouldn't make it. I believe that despite
what you have been through in your life you are a strong
person. Therefore you will have to leave."

Hessu seemed to understand my point and he accepted
the verdict.

The same day I received a call from the special teacher

at the hospital. He explained to me how he had successfully worked with Hessu during the past weeks and how Hessu had made remarkable progress. He pleaded with me to call off the discharge. The next day I received a telephone call from Hessu's social worker, who told me about the many hardships in Hessu's life and about how hard she and her colleagues had worked over the years to help him become able to stand on his own feet. She was afraid that now that there was finally some progress, discharge might be a setback he would not be able cope with. I was in a difficult spot. To give in to the pleadings of the teacher and the child welfare worker would have meant taking back my words about my belief in Hessu's strength. I decided to assemble a meeting with all the people involved. Present at this gathering were Hessu, the child welfare worker, the teacher, some members of staff and myself. I listened to everyone's point of view, but stood by my decision; I stated, once again, that to refrain from discharging Hessu would indicate that we did not believe in his strength. For that reason the only possible course of action was to go ahead with the discharge.

Hessu left after a few days. I didn't hear anything about him until some years later when I met the social worker who was then working as an alcohol counselor. She told me that after Hessu had been discharged he had been placed temporarily in a guest house where his room was paid for by child welfare. In spite of her initial apprehensions, Hessu had actually taken increasing responsibility for his own life after his discharge. When she last heard from Hessu, he was both attending vocational training and working.

The view that past traumatic experiences are a source of problems in later life is certainly plausible—at least here in the West. The opposite view that past ordeals are valuable learning experiences is equally sensible. The following example, told by Ben, dates back a number of years and illustrates this point.

Imagination in the Cupboard

Flora was referred to Ben for therapy because of depression and constant weeping. She was struggling with a number of problems, all of them related to her two sons and her ex-husband. Flora was successful in her professional life. In her work with children she was respected for her creativity and her talent for establishing contact with children.

Flora talked about her life. She spoke about her father, whom she had loved dearly but whom she rarely saw. Sometimes her father had taken her with him on his business trips; thinking about these trips still brought her joy. Flora's feelings about her mother were mixed. Her mother's excessive drinking had caused her to be ashamed of her mother throughout her childhood.

Flora said that up until now she had not shared with anyone her childhood experience of her mother. With tears running down her cheeks she revealed that when her mother was drunk she used to shut her in a dark cupboard for long periods of time.

I sympathized with her and asked, "What did you do there in that dark cupboard? How did you pass the time?"

With a miserable look on her face she explained that she used to make up all kinds of imaginary creatures to play with.

"How wonderful," I said, "Do you think that perhaps what you used to do in the cupboard is responsible for the skill you now have with children?"

Flora laughed through her tears as she suddenly became able to see her past in this tragicomic light.

Sometimes people are convinced beyond question that a particular wrongdoing, either committed by themselves onto another person or by another person onto them, is responsible for their suffering. Fortunately, guilt from having done harm to others or bitterness from having been the subject of injustice can be worked with in various ways.

For example, a physician suffered from intense guilt due to the fact that he had mistakenly administered incorrect medication during the resuscitation of a patient whose imminent death, according to her colleagues, could not have been prevented. Many of her colleagues had tried to explain that the patient died of massive heart infarction and that anything she had done or left undone was unrelated to the fact that the patient died. However much they tried to reassure her, it was of no avail. Every day she was tormented by feelings of intense guilt and the fear that God would punish her.

In order to help this doctor overcome her guilt she was given the task of writing a letter of apology to the deceased patient. She was to write the letter for herself; it was not to be sent anywhere. She felt the task was too upsetting and refused to undertake it, but she offered instead to write a letter to the deceased patient's spouse. She brought this letter to our subsequent meeting and said that she now felt ready to write the letter to the patient. In the next session she read aloud a moving letter of apology to the deceased patient. Therapy continued for several more sessions, but it appeared that the writing of the letters played a central role in her eventual recovery.

The following case, provided by Ben, involves a lawyer who sought help because of depression and intense feelings of guilt.

The Guilty Lawyer

Heikki, a lawyer in his thirties, suffered from agonizing depression. The most pressing problem was that he was convinced that one day he would be arrested for incorrect practice he had performed while working several years earlier in a judicial court in another town. He claimed that he had inadvertently made a number of mistakes in his work during that time and that he was now living in constant fear that some day his "crimes" would come out in the open. He believed he was doomed to be imprisoned and lose his profession for good.

Whatever incorrect practices Heikki had actually performed, it was evident that they were insignificant items that had not caused anybody any harm. His "crimes" involved deviating from the rules concerning how trials should be documented. The chance that anybody would ever be interested in looking for his mistakes, let alone in charging him with them, was zero. Even if this were to happen he had apparently done nothing to warrant anything more than an admonition. This fact did not have any calming influence on Heikki. His preoccupation with his alleged incorrect practice and his fantasies about the consequences took up most of his time and caused him to cry a lot. Many times he had seriously thought of voluntarily giving himself up to the police.

The theme of crime and punishment paved the way to a more general discussion about guilt and wrongdoing. Heikki was an only child who had been raised in a children's home until the age of seven. At that point his mother, who had been struggling to make ends meet on her own, took over his upbringing. Over the years Heikki had gradually become his mother's caretaker. For example, when he was a teenager and all the other boys went out dancing, Heikki, not wanting to disappoint his mother, stayed at home and kept her company. When he finally left home to study law in another town, he felt like a traitor. Even though he traveled several hundred kilometers almost every weekend to see her, he felt guilty every time he left her.

One day his mother became ill and had to be taken into hospital. He went to see her and found that although she had been in a weak condition when admitted to the hospital she was now making good progress. A few days after he returned to the university campus he was informed that his mother had died. Heikki still felt guilty about not having been present when she had needed him most and he was convinced that he was responsible for her death. I tried to persuade him to think differently, but without success.

As I saw it, Heikki had four alternatives. First, he could rethink his mother's death and, instead of accusing himself of being uncaring, blame his mother for having been too dependent on him. Second, he could atone for his sin by punishing himself. He should see to it that he suffered until, in the eyes of God, he had hurt himself enough. Third, he could repent for his sin by carrying out volunteer work to help others until he had done enough to feel able to forgive himself. The fourth alternative was to let bygones be bygones, but I warned him that this alternative was the most difficult of all.

When Heikki came to the next session he announced that he had been thinking about the four choices and that he was unable to decide what to do. He was, however, sure that neither the first alternative, that of blaming his mother, nor the second, that of suffering, were suitable for him. Heikki's determined rejection of these two alternatives not only helped him to stop blaming himself for his mother's death but also put an end to his preoccupation about his supposed incorrect practice.

Resentment, or intense and persistent rage arising from the feeling of having been wronged, can (not unlike guilt) become an obstacle to the enjoyment of one's life. The ultimate answer to persistent resentment is forgiveness, but as we all know this is often easier said than done.

The following example, by Tapani, involves a young woman who had experienced rejection in her recent past. Her rage about what had happened was so fierce that she could think of nothing but suicide. One of the many phases in her successful recovery involved being given the opportunity to fantasize about revenge.

The Revengeful Suicide

A woman named Eeva called me and wanted to make an appointment for her friend Nina, a young woman in her late thirties, who had recently tried to kill herself three

times by taking an overdose of tranquilizers. Eeva had
tried to talk with Nina, keep an eye on her, and encourage
her to seek outside help. Nina, who said she was determined to kill herself, had so far categorically refused to
meet any professional. I made an appointment for the
next day and asked the women to come to see me together.

When we met I learned that Nina was, in fact, preoccupied by suicidal thoughts. Eeva told me that Nina had
recently been abandoned by her boyfriend, with whom she
had been living and with whom she had been going steady
since they left school. Nina explained that she had devot-
ed her life to this man; she proclaimed that she had turned
him from a timid boy into a man; she had even paid for his
university education. Just when he was about to get his
first job, he suddenly left her for another woman. Nina
said she had no reason to continue living and that her
suicide would be right for him.

Our conversation resulted in an agreement that it was
not safe for Nina to be at home all by herself and so we
decided that she would move in with Eeva and her husband for the time being. We arranged to meet again the
following week.

After four days I received an unexpected phone call
from Eeva. She told me that Nina had moved in with her
as we had planned, but that on the third day she had
asked to go home in order to pick up some things. When
she did not return within the designated time Eeva tried
to call her, but there was no answer. She and her husband
drove to Nina's house and found her intoxicated, lying in
the bathtub preparing to take her life by means of an
electric shock. They took her to an emergency clinic and
the next day she was transferred to a psychiatric hospital.

After this phone call from Eeva I called Nina at the
hospital and found that the only thing that interested her
at that moment was how to be released.

"How do I get discharged?" she asked me.

"If you want to get out you have to promise not to kill yourself," I explained.

"But I have no reason to live," she said.

I knew that I had a very slim chance of convincing her about the marvels life might bring so I decided to take a different path.

"I can give you one reason to stay alive," I said.

"Yeah, and what would that be?" said Nina in a cynical tone of voice.

"You could live for my sake?"

"What?"

"Well," I said, "we therapists work hard to earn our reputations. If you now take your life that would be very bad publicity for me."

"You're crazy!" she snapped back with a touch of amusement in her voice.

"Maybe, but speaking honestly, I dislike the thought of your killing yourself. If there is no reason in the whole world for you to live, you can at least stay alive for my sake."

"OK, but if I stay alive it doesn't solve the problem," Nina explained, "my life is miserable and will continue to be that way."

"I promise to try and help you make your life less miserable. However, I have to admit that I haven't been of much help so far. Is there anybody else who could help you? How about your parents?" I asked.

"I don't want to have anything to do with them," said Nina. "The only person who can help me is Jari (the ex-boyfriend), but he refuses to talk to me."

"I can promise to speak with him and ask him to come and talk with you. Would you like me to do that?"

"Yes I would, but I don't believe he'll do it."

I called Jari the same day. I told him about what had happened and said that Nina needed to talk to him. He explained that he had tried to talk with Nina on several occasions after their separation, but that on each occasion Nina had become hysterical, accusing him of ruining her life. In spite of this he agreed to go and see her at the hospital. When he arrived Nina, once again, started accusing him so furiously that the staff had to intervene. Finally Nina and Jari sat together on her bed sobbing and embracing each other for half an hour.

A week later, when Nina was being released from the hospital, she called me to make an appointment. Instead of seeing her at my office in town, I decided to ask her to travel some 50 kilometers out of town to see me. She was curious to know why I wanted her to do this. I explained that there is a healing river near my house. She agreed to come and we fixed a date.

A few days later we were walking down a trail to the small river that runs past my house. To my surprise Nina pulled a camera out of her bag. She wanted to take a picture of the healing river.

It was early spring and my humble stream looked rather gloomy. The muddy water was at a low level and chunks of ice were floating slowly downstream. Scattered stained patches of snow lay on the banks and everything looked gray, as the leaves had not started to come out.

"This looks terrible!" Nina cried out.

"Yes it does," I had to admit. Then I added, "It will stay that way as well."

"No it won't," said Nina without thinking. "I know very well that spring is coming and soon it will look pretty."

"You never know," I replied, "we may have a second winter with the greenhouse effect and everything!"

"Come on, I know spring is well on the way."

This amused me and I couldn't help showing it.

"What are you laughing at?" Nina said.

"I don't know. I'm amused by this situation," I tried to explain.

"Aha, so this is some kind of metaphor," she said shaking her head knowingly.

As we walked back up to the house we started talking about the future. I told Nina that in my view she now had at least three choices.

"First, you can become a bitch," I said. "You know, the kind of bitter woman who lives alone, never enjoying anything, wearing drab clothes, thinking about nothing but her misfortune, and yet living to a very old age."

Nina was unimpressed by this scenario and asked me about the second choice.

"Second you can seek revenge," I said and observed that she became visibly intrigued by the idea. I discussed the clever ways in which the characters in TV soap operas retaliate and suggested that perhaps Nina could do something similar. "You could ruin his life, jeopardize his professional career, or destroy his relationship with the new woman by spreading nasty rumors about him. How about it?"

Nina smiled and said that this was the best choice so far, but it wasn't her style to seek revenge on people.

"The third choice," I explained, "involves forgiving Jari for what he has done. This alternative requires you to think of a way in which he could compensate you for the suffering he has caused if, one day in the future, he might be willing to so do."

As I drove Nina back to the railway station I recommended that she go to her parents, tell them of the options we had discussed, and ask them to help her choose what she wanted for her future.

Two months later I spoke with Nina on the phone and learned that soon after our meeting she had indeed gone to see her parents. Their meeting had started with her parents criticizing her. She had reacted by screaming and threatening to leave. Gradually everyone had calmed down and, to use her own words, Nina had talked sincerely with her parents for the first time in years.

Nina had then recovered gradually, she had found herself a new job and even returned to her studies.

Since I had not charged her for the most recent consultation, she asked me what she owed me. I said that if she felt any debt of gratitude to me, she could perhaps do me a favor. She said she would be glad to help and asked how.

I said, "If in the future I encounter clients who are determined to kill themselves in the way that you were, may I
ask for your help?"

"Sure, but how could I possibly be of help?" she said.

"By telling them your story, the story of how you survived," I said.

She agreed.

The idea that problems are caused by unresolved grief has
occupied a central role in Western psychology. Based on this
belief clients have been encouraged to talk about and "work
through" their past losses.

Ben once received a telephone call from a woman who had
recently lost her husband in a car accident. A psychologist
friend of hers who had visited the home had remarked that the
daughter was coping well, as she was expressing her emotion
by crying and being angry. He had, however, been concerned
about the son, who was not displaying any strong feelings, did
not particularly wish to talk about the accident, and appeared
only slightly perturbed. The psychologist had said that the boy
was in need of therapy. The mother then called Ben to consult
him about the need for therapy. He gave her an opportunity to
relate what had happened and how each family member was
managing. The discussion led to the view that each family
member had his or her own personal style of coping with the
loss and that the son's reaction could also be seen as normal
and appropriate. We agreed to monitor the situation without
further therapy. After some months the mother informed Ben
that in her opinion this had been the right decision.

The following description is from a consultation session we
did in a workshop for professionals in a small town in Finland.
It illustrates many facets of solution talk, such as focusing on
the future, building on previous progress, and sharing one's
own experiences with clients. Early in the conversation it
emerged that the client had lost a child. The issue was deliberately set aside until later. When it was brought up again to-

wards the end of the session, the loss of the child was discussed in what could be defined as a solution-oriented manner.

Reassurance from Heaven

Maria, a middle-aged woman who had suffered from depression for three years and had been disabled from work for one and a half years, was invited to a consultation by Henrik, her psychiatrist. Maria had been asked to choose whether there was someone she wanted to accompany her and she brought Pirjo, her neighbor and friend.

We started the session by asking Henrik what he would like to be the result of the session. His objective was that Maria would gain sufficient confidence to start working again and subsequently realize that she is happier if she is working. Maria seemed to agree with this goal but Pirjo remarked that it was equally important for Maria to feel happier at home.

"Do you think it is befitting to say that Maria is now at a crossroads in her life?" asked Ben. Since everyone seemed to agree with this description, he continued, "Several roads lead away from here. One road leads to a place in which Maria is unhappy at work and unhappy at home. Another one leads to a place where Maria is happy at work, but not so happy at home. And a third road leads to a place where Maria is happy both at home and at work. Would you agree, Maria, that the task of this consultation is to help you go down the right road?"

"Just a minute," interjected Tapani, "I want to check whether Maria feels herself to be at the crossroads or whether, perhaps, she feels that she has passed it and is already traveling on the right road? Is there any indication that you are already on the right road?"

"I believe there is," said Henrik, "Maria is going out and has made plans to return to work."

"I recently visited my former workplace for the first time in three years," Maria explained, "and I'm now planning to start work in two weeks' time. I have always been keen to work even though I have suffered from arthritis all my life. When I was only 17 the doctors recommended me for a permanent disability pension but I didn't want it. I have always worked . . . " At this point she paused and then, with tears in her eyes she continued, "until my son died at the age of 18 three years ago."

We decided to adhere to our forward-looking approach in spite of this information about the tragic death of a child in the past. Ben continued by asking, "How about your husband? Has he observed any signs of progress? Does Pirjo have any idea what he might say?"

"He would say that Maria has started to take care of her appearance," said Pirjo.

"You mean that she has started to use makeup?" asked Tapani.

"Yes, but that's only a part of it. Now she also goes to the hairdresser."

"Is there something else worth mentioning here?" asked Tapani.

Henrik said, "Maria's mood is much better and she has been looking for someone to take care of her toddler when she starts working. Recently she has even been laughing occasionally. I truly admire her determination to return to work."

"I'm curious to know," Ben asked Henrik, "what it is that you two have been talking about?"

"Mostly we have been talking about flowers," said Henrik, provoking laughter in the group. "I mean it. You wouldn't believe what a tremendous green thumb she has."

We continued the session by letting Maria give credit to the various people who had already been of help to her and by fantasizing about Maria's future life. Towards the end of the session we returned to the death in the family.

"You mentioned that you lost one of your children," Ben said. "How many children do you have?"

A silence filled the room. We learned only later that almost everyone present, except us, knew about the tragedy. Maria's son had died late one night in a traffic accident. The accident had been a shock to the whole town and had been widely discussed. Only Maria had not wanted to talk about it.

"My oldest son was 18 when he died in a traffic accident," said Maria. "My second son is 15 and my little one is only two."

"How have you managed to recover from the shock?" asked Ben.

As tears filled her eyes Maria said, "I don't think I have recovered. When a young person is taken away just like that, it is something I believe one never really recovers from. You constantly think about it. If only we hadn't bought him the car, if only we hadn't told him to come home from his friend's house that night."

"Have you blamed yourself for the accident?" asked Ben.

"I have blamed myself and I have blamed my husband."

"Understanding what it feels like to lose one's child is probably something other people can never really do unless, of course, they have themselves experienced something similar," said Ben. "I wonder if there is anybody else here in the group who has had to face something of this kind and who would like to share their experience with Maria?"

Two people volunteered their stories. A young mental health worker described how his brother had died when he himself was only nine. An elderly nurse told of the death of her adult son several years ago. She said that her recovery started when she finally gave up thinking about how his death might have been avoided.

"Would you say, Maria, that you have begun to move away from blaming yourself and thinking about how the accident could have been avoided?" asked Ben.

"The pain is still there," said Maria.

"Do you feel, like some people do, that time is the only thing that can heal this kind of wound?" asked Tapani.

"Yes," agreed Maria.

"Do you have any idea how long it will take for you to overcome the pain?" said Tapani.

"It will take another three years," said Maria.

"I wonder if there is anything to be done to make the time shorter," continued Tapani. "Suppose we could ask your son. We might imagine that your son would descend from heaven in the form of an angel and join our conversation. If he had been listening and we were able to ask him to tell us what he thinks should be done, what do you imagine he would say, Maria?"

After a moment of silence Maria said, "He would say, 'You just go to work, mother, and take care of yourself.'"

We then drew the session to a close. Just as we were about to finish, Maria said, "I have been wondering about the medication. Is it really necessary?"

"Do you want us to persuade Henrik to take you off medication?" asked Ben with a smile.

"I don't know, but there have been ups and downs and I have noticed that the medication doesn't seem to make any difference."

"All right, you persuaded me," said Henrik warmly, and we ended the session.

When we met Henrik two years later at a seminar he told us that after this consultation there had been no further sessions with Maria but she had maintained contact with him by phone. Maria had started working as she had planned, and she used medication occasionally. She used to say, "Little by little, I'm doing better and better."

Even if solution talk tends to be focused on the future rather than the past, this does not mean that the talking about the past should become a forbidden or even an undesirable topic. The past does not need to be discussed in terms of the source of troubles but as a resource. One can learn to see one's past misfortunes as ordeals that, in addition to having caused suffering, have also brought about something valuable and worthwhile.

It should be emphasized that the view that adverse life events — even being victimized — can later, in hindsight, be seen as valuable learning experiences does not in any way justify violence, abuse, or neglect. In making this point we have often used the metaphor of healing bones: Even if fractured bones may sometimes become stronger after healing, it does not justify fracturing bones. However strong a bone may become from recovering from an accidental fracture we do all in our power to protect ourselves and others from such injury.

3

MAKING AND UNMAKING CONNECTIONS

Often when people come to professionals for help they present initially with a single, clear-cut difficulty that they wish to solve. For example, a patient may come to see a doctor complaining initially about a headache. As the assessment proceeds, the doctor finds out that the patient has problems in her love life, is confused about religious matters, quarrels with her mother, suffers from insomnia, and indulges occasionally in binge eating. When entering the doctor's office the patient carries with her the problem in a plastic bag — upon leaving she is stooped over with the weight of numerous plastic bags each one with another problem.

This state of affairs poses a dilemma for the therapist: How should one think about the relationship between several simultaneous problems? Does one of them cause the others, and if so, which is the cause and which are the effects? Should all the problems perhaps be seen as symptoms of yet another underlying problem still to be discovered? Is it possible for each of the simultaneous problems to be independent and unrelated to the others?

For example, a child attending kindergarten, school, or a residential treatment home has behavioral problems. It is known that there are various problems within the child's family. In such instances it has been customary to assume that problems at the institution are caused by problems at home.

Connecting problems at home and problems at the institution is, however, not the only plausible view. It could also be assumed that there simply happen to exist two simultaneous but separate problems, one in the home and another at the institution, without either one causing the other. Still another possibility is to turn the tables and claim that problems at home are caused by problems at the institution. After all, it is not uncommon for children's problems outside the family to become a source of heated conflicts inside the family. Favoring a particular view of the way in which the problems are linked may, for better or worse, have an influence on achieving the desired change.

The following example, which dates back to the first year of our training seminars, illustrates how ideas for solving a problem can begin to flow more freely simply through challenging the presumed causal link between the presenting problem and another, coexisting problem.

The Tin Man

Santtu was a 10-year-old boy who refused to go to school. When his father was about to leave the schoolyard in the mornings, Santtu became overwhelmed with anxiety. Some time previously Santtu's mother had taken a one-month leave of absence from work in order to sit with him in class. This arrangement worked well, but when her leave of absence ended Santtu refused to go to school once again. The school counselor had referred the family for evaluation at the outpatient unit of a children's psychiatric hospital. At this hospital the parents had been told that Santtu's problem was associated with an underlying disturbance in the relationship between the parents. Based on this diagnosis the parents had been advised to seek family therapy. Both parents accepted this diagnosis and made an appointment for family therapy at the local child guidance center. The social worker at this center was currently training with us and decided to invite the family to a consultation.

In the pre-session discussion, which was still part of our routine at that time, it was decided that the therapy should focus on practical solutions – on what to do to get Santtu to school – rather than hypothesizing about underlying dynamics. However, when the therapist suggested this approach to the parents at the beginning of the session, they objected and argued intelligently in favor of discussing underlying problems rather than the symptom. The therapist was encouraged, through the phone, to stand by our original plan. She was advised to explain to the parents that even in medicine there are situations when the treatment of symptoms takes priority over examining the underlying disease. As an example we used an epileptic seizure, which needs to be treated symptomatically before a more thorough neurological examination is made. After a lengthy negotiation, during which the therapist convinced the parents that she would deal with their marital problems as soon as the boy was attending school, they accepted this approach.

"All right then," said father, "we will attempt to get him to go to school first, but what on earth can we do? We have already tried everything."

Gently, with the parents, the therapist reviewed all the solutions that had already been attempted and proposed that maybe there was still something else that could be tried. Finally, a plan was made to invite Santtu's teacher to the next session at the child guidance clinic and to involve her in the quest for a new way of proceeding.

The next session with the teacher proved useful. Santtu explained that he would attend school if only he weren't overcome by awful feelings of anxiety at the moment of separation. Plans were made to help Santtu learn to master his anxiety. Santtu himself came up with the idea that he could call his anxiety "The Tin Man." This nickname described Santtu's feeling empty-headed and losing control of his lower limbs. At home Santtu and his father devised methods of practicing control of these feelings until gradually Santtu became capable of turning The Tin Man voluntarily on and off. Within a couple of weeks Santtu was attending school again and everyone seemed pleased with the situation.

At the next session the social worker, loyal to her promise, brought up the question of the presumed underlying marital problem, "As was agreed, we'll now begin to work on the issues between the two of you," she explained.

"Well," said the father, "things have actually been quite well between us lately, haven't they, darling?"

"Yes, I agree. I can't presently see any particular issues that need to be discussed."

"But . . . " insisted the social worker, "we all agreed that we would concentrate on your relationship as soon as the school problem was solved."

At this point Santtu interjected, "Perhaps you should discuss your problems now," he said in a mature manner, "You see, if you don't, my problem may return."

The social worker was amused by Santtu's astuteness, but the parents simply looked at him and said firmly, "No, it won't return!"

Marital issues were never discussed in therapy and Santtu's problem did not recur.

In the final analysis, it is often impossible to know for sure whether a given problem is, or is not, caused by another particular problem. However, from the pragmatic point of view, it may be best to assume that there need not be any causal connection between two concomitant problems. In this way it becomes possible to focus on solving the actual complaint rather than the presumed underlying problems. Solving the complaint in a collaborative manner can be a positive experience that reflects favorably on other subsequent problems as well.

The following example is drawn from Ben's time as a consultant for a child guidance clinic. Thanks to the fact that he had no advance information about the case, he was able to avoid becoming embroiled in the other problems of the family. Instead, he focused on solving the presenting problem. Had he been aware of the supposed underlying problem, this kind of a solution might not have emerged.

The Resourceful Boy's Promise

Iiro, a nine-year-old school boy, came in with his mother for consultation. As is usual, I had not received any information about the case before I started the interview. I found out from the mother that Iiro had been absent from school without a legitimate excuse for a large number of days in the current year. He usually pretended to go to school in the morning, but as soon as his parents had left the house he returned home. On occasions when he didn't return home, he roamed the streets and hung around with various dubious people in the town center.

"And what do you do all day long when you are at home? Is it boring to be at home all alone?" I asked Iiro, beginning to make contact with him.

"I watch TV," said Iiro.

"But there's nothing on during the day, is there?"

"We have the saucer. I watch Sky channel."

"Aha, so you have the satellite. You must be an expert on music videos then. By the way, they speak English on Sky channel. Have you learned to understand what they say?"

"Yes."

"That's a great way to learn English!"

I directed my next question to the mother and the therapist involved with the case, "Has there been any progress lately?"

"Yes," said the mother proudly, "Iiro has attended gymnastics lessons."

"That's great. How did you do that?" I asked Iiro.

He just shook his shoulders, but his mother was proud to explain, "Iiro and his gym teacher had a conversation, with the result that Iiro promised to attend gym lessons."

"How good," I said and turned to back to Iiro, "It seems as if you are a man of your word. Am I right?"

"What does that mean?" asked Iiro.

"It means that if you make a promise then you keep it. Are you like that?"

"Yes, I am."

"That's fine. Would you also be willing to promise that you will attend the other lessons as well?"

"Why not," said Iiro.

I thought to myself that this was a bit too good to be true, but suspected, not unlike everyone else in the room, that even if Iiro now committed himself to going to school he might not stick to it for very long.

"I like your style," I said and pointed to a video camera that was attached to the wall. "You see that video camera over there. It's not switched on right now but we could turn it on and record your promise on video. Would you agree to that?"

"Yes," said Iiro enthusiastically. He was presumably seeing himself on the TV screen.

"We could then let your teacher and perhaps your whole class see you on TV. How does that sound to you?"

Iiro agreed to this proposal and his mother and the therapist had nothing against it either. Within a few minutes the video recording was made and we all gathered in the observation room to look at it. There was Iiro, proudly making his TV promise that he would from then on attend school, not only gymnastics lessons but everything else as well. After we had looked at the clip Iiro suddenly announced that he needed to leave.

"Where are you going?" asked his mother.

"I'm late for school," said Iiro as he hurried away from the office.

The rest of us went back to the therapy room and continued with the session.

"What a resourceful son you have," I said to the mother. "I have rarely seen anybody as enterprising as him in my career. He's quite something."

"Yes, I know he is resourceful," said Iiro's mother, holding the newly recorded video in her lap, "but the actual problem is that my husband refuses to come here."

"Why would you want him to come here?" I asked.

"Iiro's problems are caused by my husband's drinking. He drinks beer and when he starts he cannot stop. He goes out with his friends and stays with them for days in a row. He won't agree to come here even though I have asked him many times."

"So you want him to come here with you to discuss his drinking because you trust the people here. I have great confidence in them, too, so it is probably a good idea to get him to come. Obviously I cannot know why he refuses to come here, but if I put myself in his shoes, and I'm a father too, I can imagine that he is afraid that if he were to come here he would be blamed for Iiro's problems. Do you think that might be possible?"

"Perhaps."

"In that case it might be helpful if we could somehow reassure him that he will not actually be blamed. Could you tell him that in my judgment Iiro is an extremely resourceful boy and that I'm thinking that he might have inherited this characteristic from his father. Something else which might be worth mentioning to your husband is that he has probably been wise to stay away from home during his drinking binges. In that way Iiro doesn't have see him when he is drunk and that may have contributed to Iiro's resourcefulness. If you give this message to your husband he may reconsider joining you here in the future. How about it?"

"Maybe," said mother.

I changed the subject, "What about the video? What will you do with it?"

"I guess we'll first take a look at it at home. I could then give it to Iiro's teacher at school."

"That's fine. My suggestion is that you let the teacher decide what she wants to do with it, whether she wants to show it to the class or just view it herself with or without Iiro."

"Yes, she can decide for herself," agreed mother as we ended the session.

I later learned from the therapist that Iiro had, indeed, gone directly to school from our session. He also kept his videotaped promise and no longer missed lessons at school. The therapist continued meeting the family and felt more optimistic about getting the father to participate in future sessions.

In the previous examples the possible causal links between two problems were challenged or ignored. Another approach to handling situations where there are two supposedly linked problems is that of turning the tables by reversing the cause and effect. Turning supposedly causal relationships upside-down is a way of discovering totally new ways of dealing with problems. For example, it is often assumed that low self-esteem causes various problems. The opposite view, that problems cause low self-esteem is actually equally plausible but requires a different approach. Psychological problems are assumed to cause excessive consumption of alcohol, but in such cases it is also possible to think that psychological problems result from drinking. Hallucinatory voices are generally seen as a symptom of schizophrenia, but schizophrenia may also be considered as a reaction to hearing hallucinatory voices.

The following example, by Tapani, illustrates the reversal of alleged causality. The family was seen a number of years ago at a child guidance center.

Fishing Buddies

Ismo was a 9-year-old boy whose mother had died a couple of years earlier. Since his mother's death Ismo had had a variety of problems, which had all been explained as symptoms of his anxiety. For example, he no longer played with his friends and stayed at home close to his father for all his free time. He refused to go to school

unless his father took him there in the morning and collected him in the afternoon. When this was impossible
Ismo sat at home all day doing nothing.

Father explained that Ismo acted as if he were glued to
him. For example, if father went to another room in the
house Ismo immediately became upset and asked, "Dad-
dy, where are you going?" Father was exceedingly understanding of Ismo and explained that he himself had also
suffered from intense anxiety after his wife's death. Every
evening Ismo and his father sat together at home and
spent their time watching TV while consuming large
quantities of food. Not surprisingly, both of them were
considerably overweight.

"Tell me, what would the two of you be doing if you
didn't have that anxiety?" I asked father.

"Well, I guess we'd do the things we used to do,
wouldn't we?" said father.

"Yeah," agreed Ismo.

"I'd be interested to know what you used to do. Ismo,
can you tell me?"

"Yes. We visited people, and we went swimming at the
pool at least once a week. Dad and I also used to go
fishing in our local lake," Ismo explained.

"At times it may be hard to say which comes first," I
begun to explain. "Does the anxiety prevent one from doing things, or does one become anxious because one isn't
doing anything? Doing nothing certainly allows one plenty of time to think about matters which produce anxiety."

Both father and son looked perplexed. I continued,
"Luckily, in your case there is a way to find out which
comes first. I suggest that you go swimming as you used
to despite your anxiety and see what happens. That way
you can find out which way it is for yourself."

Both Ismo and his father agreed to follow through with
the experiment. I found out later that during the next few
weeks they not only had gone swimming but had also
visited relatives and had even gone fishing together.

Not only therapists but also medical doctors face the question of how to think about the possible connections between simultaneous problems. A common notion within psychosomatic medicine is the idea of psychogenesis, the belief that somatic ailments are symptomatic of underlying psychological problems. This idea, currently exceedingly popular among the general public, is not without its drawbacks. To imply that the mind is responsible for causing problems in the body results in an odd state of affairs, where two parts of the person are judged to be in conflict with each other.

A more fruitful psychosomatic approach is to see mind and body as partners, as friends caring for and helping each other. Instead of assuming that the mind imposes its own problems onto the body, it is more helpful to think that the mind supports the body in its tasks of coping with pain and discomfort, healing wounds, and regenerating tissue.

In the following example Tapani proposes the idea that body and mind care for each other to a client who is suffering from stomach pain.

Body and Mind as Allies

Pelle had experienced several months of gastritis. His abdominal pain and discomfort were so severe that the illness preoccupied him for most of his waking hours. He had seen many physicians and also various natural healers, including an osteopath and an acupuncturist, with minimal results. He had finally become convinced that his problem was psychosomatic.

During a telephone conversation with Pelle I told him, "It may well be that your problem is psychosomatic. If it is, I want to tell you what I think about the idea of psychosomatics. I like to think of body and mind as friends who are determined to help each other."

"I follow you," he said.

"All right then, let us assume that your mind is using

your stomach to remind you of something. For example, it could be that something important for your well-being is lacking in your life right now. It may be something you have neglected, or an important aspiration in your life that you have ignored lately. Suppose your stomach could speak and you could ask it what it wants to tell you? What do you suppose it would say? Will you think about it?"

I later learned that Pelle still saw his problem as psychosomatic but that he had adopted the view that his stomach was trying to help him. With the help of a naturopath he gradually recovered from his problem.

When two simultaneous problems exist, it becomes possible for a therapist to propose a plan in which one problem is utilized in solving another. An interesting example of this idea has been provided by Cloé Madanes. In one of her lectures she told of a family where the daughter suffered from severe anorexia and the father engaged in continuous heavy drinking. In the first session, which was a house call, the therapist succeeded in negotiating an agreement between father and daughter according to which the daughter promised to start eating if the father stopped drinking and the father promised to stop drinking if the daughter started eating. This agreement proved useful in starting therapy with the otherwise reluctant girl.

Another example of linking two problems together in a fruitful way is known as ordeal therapy. This approach was originally described by Milton Erickson and later elaborated by Jay Haley (Haley, 1984). It involves making a contract with the client that relates another difficulty to the presenting problem. In the contract the client agrees to work on the difficulty in proportion to the extent to which the presenting problem appears. Tapani applied this strategy in the following vignette.

Sherry and Cleaning

Several years ago, when I was working full time as the director of alcohol and drug abuse services, I once visited a woman who following her divorce had been drinking a whole bottle of sherry every evening. She was not the least troubled by her drinking; in fact, she only complained that her house was in such a mess that when she came home from work she was filled with self-reproach. After having talked with her for a while I asked if she would be willing to hear my suggestions.

"If it involves my having to stop drinking, don't bother," she said.

"No, no," I replied, "if you accept my suggestion you can continue to drink sherry, but you will get your house clean."

"That sounds like something for me," she said.

"OK, the proposal is that starting tomorrow you go and buy your sherry bottle after work as usual. You come home, pour yourself a glass of sherry and sit down and drink it slowly. After you have finished the first glass you clean the house for a quarter of an hour. Then you can have your second glass of sherry. After the second glass you clean again for a quarter of an hour, and so on until the bottle is empty or you've had enough. This way you don't have to stop drinking but you won't have to suffer from a bad conscience for not taking care of your house."

She not only agreed to the plan but also followed through with it. When her house was clean and tidy she made an important decision concerning her ex-husband which she had been postponing. Soon afterwards she gave up her detrimental drinking habit.

Of all the various ways of connecting problems to one another, the most helpful is that of seeing the different problems as helping in the solving of one another.

In the following example, drawn from one of Ben's workshops, this idea is employed in discussing with a therapist from an adolescent counseling center the case of a teenager who had come for counselling after being raped.

Incest and Rape

A therapist asked for advice in helping a girl who had initiated contact with the center soon after having been raped by an acquaintance of hers. After a few sessions of counselling the girl had revealed that there was an important "issue" concerning her father but that she was not yet ready to talk about it. Her statement had given rise to the suspicion that she had been sexually abused by her father. The therapist wondered about how to proceed in order to get the girl to talk about what had happened with her father.

The suspicion of incest shifted the focus of therapy from dealing with the rape to attempts to explore the possibility of incest. However, this approach was not to the client's liking. No matter how hard the therapist tried, the girl did not disclose any further information concerning the father. As the therapist did not think there was enough evidence to warrant notifying the child welfare authorities, he didn't know how to proceed with the case.

We suggested that the two problems, the rape and the possible incest, should not be seen as connected to one another and engaged the workshop participants in a conversation about how to proceed in accordance with this view.

The following suggestion emerged from the discussion. The therapist should feel free to set aside the problem of possible incest for the time being and continue to focus on helping the girl to find a way to deal with the recent rape. If the therapist were to succeed in helping the girl to confront the boy who raped her, this experience would give her courage to disclose the possible incest. Some people in the group observed that since the rapist was one of her peers there was, at least in theory, the possibility of arranging a session between the girl and the boy who was guilty of the sexual offense. A face-to-face session, involving negotiation about how the boy could atone for the pain he had caused, could be useful for both parties. The therapist accepted this as a way to proceed.

When we saw the therapist some time later he informed us that not long after our workshop session the girl had disclosed that her father had sexually abused her and that therapy was continuing.

In families where there are multiple problems, there is a temptation for professionals to link the problems together so that distinct problems are seen as causing, maintaining, or complicating each other.

In the following example, a single mother had major difficulties with two of her teenage daughters. Up until the time of the consultation the predominant view of mother and professionals involved with the case had been that the sisters were a bad influence on each other. We adopted the opposite view, according to which the fact that both sisters had problems made them well qualified to help each other.

Pia, Heidi, and Friends

A social worker from a short-term residential home for adolescents (The House), invited two sisters, Pia and Heidi, to our seminar together with their mother. The mother had experienced insurmountable problems with these two daughters, particularly 12-year-old Pia. Pia was playing truant, used alcohol with her friends, did not comply with her mother's curfew, and often stayed out all night without informing her mother of her whereabouts. Heidi, who was 17, had similar problems. She fought constantly with her mother and particularly with her mother's current live-in boyfriend. The third daughter in the family, aged 13, had none of the problems of her two sisters.

Three months previously the child protection officer and mother had agreed that the situation with Pia and

Heidi had deteriorated to the point where the two girls could no longer live at home. The social worker subsequently placed the two sisters temporarily in The House. As the girls had already stayed the maximum possible time (three months), the staff at The House now felt it was high time for the girls to move on. We also learned that, although both girls had liked their stay at The House, Pia had continued to have the same problems as she used to have at home. She had not obeyed her curfew and there had been nights when she had not come back at all.

We invited the family members and the social worker to imagine what would constitute a desirable result for our conversation.

Pia said, "I would be allowed to return home."

Heidi said, "I would be able to decide where to go." She explained that she had several choices. She was not even considering moving back to live with her mother. Her options included moving in with her father, moving in with her uncle's family, or moving to another residential home for adolescents where she would have the opportunity to work.

Mother said, "Pia would realize that she can eventually come home, but that she needs to go to another residential home first. She has to change her ways before she can come back home." Pia protested loudly about being sent to another residential home.

The social worker said, "I agree with mother — Pia needs to understand that she has to spend some time in another institution before she can return home."

"What would you say," said Tapani to Pia, "if I were to be your advocate and try to convince your mother and the social worker to let you go straight home?"

"That suits me fine," said Pia, "because I am not going to go to an institution anyway. If they force me to go there, I won't obey any rules at all and I'll have to stay there forever!"

"All right, then let's see what would be the conditions under which you could go straight home without having to go to the institution first," said Tapani. He then turned to the mother and asked her, "Would you take Pia home for a one-week trial period if the staff from The House were able to inform you that they have had no problems at all with her for a period of, say, two weeks?"

"That's the problem! I know that she hasn't been obeying the rules at The House."

"OK, she hasn't up until now," said Tapani. "But let's suppose – and this is just a thought experiment – that we could succeed in devising a plan which worked so well that Pia would fully comply with the rules of The House. If this were possible, would you take her home for a trial period?"

"Yes, if she would behave for two weeks I would certainly take her home for a trial period. Why not?" said mother.

"How many times do I have to tell you that if I am allowed to go home I will obey the rules?" Pia shouted.

"I cannot believe her," explained mother. "She has promised to follow the rules so many times before but she never keeps her promises."

"Does Pia listen to you?" asked Tapani.

"No she doesn't. She doesn't give a damn about what I say," answered mother.

"Does she take more notice of her big sister?" continued Tapani.

"She surely does and that's a problem because Heidi has exactly the same problems that she has," said mother. "Heidi is a very bad example to Pia. They shouldn't be together."

"You'll never succeed in separating us," yelled Heidi resentfully.

Ignoring the conflict, Tapani continued talking to mother. "OK, but let's suppose that for one reason or another Heidi actually ordered Pia to follow the rules. Would she then obey?"

"I know that Pia does obey Heidi, but as long as Heidi herself continues to be a bad example I don't believe it would ever work," said mother.

"Let's suppose – and remember that we are only imagining – that Heidi not only commanded her sister to obey the rules but also changed her own behavior so that she became a good example to her sister. Do you think in that case Heidi would be able to get Pia to change her ways?"

"Yes, it would help," said mother.

At this point Tapani turned to Heidi and said to her with a twinkle in his eye, "What's your price for sacrificing your current life style and becoming a good model for your little sister?"

"I don't need to be paid anything. I'll do anything to help my sister," declared Heidi.

At this point Ben entered the discussion with the intention of identifying additional resources in Pia's social network. "Pia, could you name some of your best friends?" Pia responded without hesitation, giving the names of four of her good friends, three girls and a boy.

"Does Heidi know these friends of yours?" asked Ben.

"I know all of them quite well," said Heidi.

"Do you think they would be willing to help Pia?"

"I'm sure they would," said Heidi.

"All right then," continued Tapani and turned to the social worker, "How about you? Suppose we succeed in finding a way to help Pia change so that she obeys all the rules. Would you agree to extend her stay for an additional two-week trial period?"

"We cannot do that," declared the social worker. "Pia is moving to the other institution next Wednesday. We visited the place with her last week. It's a nice place. They even have a swimming pool there."

At this point Pia blew her top. In a tirade seasoned with an impressive array of four-letter words she once again made clear what she thought about being placed in the other institution.

After a short break we proposed that the remaining time be focused on thinking about how to help Pia make the placement at the other institution as brief as possible.

This suggestion was accepted by everyone, including Pia.

"My suggestion is," said Ben, "that we invite Heidi and some of Pia's friends to another meeting. At that meeting we can discuss how Heidi together with Pia's friends can influence Pia to behave so well that she will be allowed to return home as early as possible. Heidi, do you think that Pia's friends would be willing to come to such a meeting?"

"I believe they would," said Heidi.

"Pia, what about you, would you join us?" asked Ben.

"Sure," said Pia.

Tapani noticed that mother was being neglected, "Let's not forget mother. Would you come as well?"

"I'd rather not. I've been to so many meetings that I've simply had enough," said mother honestly.

"I think we should give mom a vacation from taking care of all these problems. Don't you think you deserve it, mom?" said Ben.

"I certainly do," said mother. We ended the session with an agreement to meet after two weeks.

A fortnight later we had a session with Heidi and two of Pia's friends. Pia had now moved to the other institution, and according to Heidi, was determined to put her life in order. Heidi explained that Pia had not come to the meeting because she didn't want to miss school. Pia had also improved her relationship with her mother and even with her mother's boyfriend. We decided to respond to all this good news by sending Pia an encouraging letter. Together with the girls we wrote the following note to Pia:

"We have been sitting here and talking with your terrific sister and really nice friends. We have heard that you have been taking good care of yourself and we feel happy for you. It's wonderful that you are going to school now and that you have improved your relationships with your mother and her boyfriend. You are lucky to have a mother, sister, and friends who have supported you in your achievement. We wish you the best of luck in your future."

It is not uncommon that several problems emerge when people consult professionals about their difficulties. Whether these problems are seen to be connected, and if so how, has a major impact on how people will come to view their own situation and how they will set about solving their problems. The act of connecting problems to one another or seeing them as causing each other often interferes with people's ability to maintain their optimism and creativity.

When multiple difficulties exist, seeing each problem as an independent element with a life of its own allows people to consider the possibility that progress in dealing with one problem may be of help in solving another.

4

WATCHFUL WORDING

Midnight Cowboy

We were teaching a group of people who worked as volunteers for an anonymous hot-line telephone service run by a church. One of the problems presented by the group involved a man who called the hot line fairly regularly. He always called a few minutes before midnight, even though he was well aware that the service closed at midnight. When he called he always seemed to be somewhat drunk and demanded to talk for a long time, often for more than an hour. He had no particular problem to present, but used the time to criticize the volunteers he had talked to previously, to make vague suicidal threats, and sometimes even to allude to the possibility of murdering someone. The volunteers, intimidated by this man, asked for our advice in dealing with him. We suggested that a useful way to start was to find a suitable name for the problem. "What words have you used to refer to this problem so far?" we asked.

"Nothing in particular. We've just used the phrase 'the aggressive caller,'" said the head of the service.

"OK, but now let's find another word to describe his behavior. The new term should fit his behavior and it should also be such that even if the man himself heard it, he would find it agreeable."

After a brief discussion in small groups the appropriate

term was found. From now on the man was to be called "The Midnight Cowboy."

Names, labels, and diagnostic concepts are more than just innocent terms used to refer to particular problems. They are also shorthand for underlying beliefs and assumptions about the nature of the problem. They refer not only to observable behavior, but also to a host of presuppositions about important questions such as severity, course, causation, and therapeutic intervention. Most terms, even those meant to be purely descriptive and etiology-free, such as words in the psychiatric classification system DSM-III-R (APA, 1987), are often loaded with presuppositions about causality and treatment.

Even the common words "disturbance," "disorder," "dysfunction," and "pathology" evoke images of abnormality and deficiency. They raise the idea that fault exists somewhere and strongly suggest that people with special training are needed to solve the problem.

Richard Belson, a family therapist from New York, reports that after completing his initial evaluation of a family with a problem child, he often informs the parents, "Your child truly has a problem that needs to be worked with, but I am pleased to tell you that in my opinion he is not disturbed." This way of describing the situation has proved to be a relief to parents. It is much better to have a child with a problem which is solvable than to have a child suffering from a disturbance which needs to be treated.

To select a particular term is to subscribe to a legion of underlying assumptions associated with that term. Words used in psychiatry and psychology (e.g., identity disorder, symbiotic psychosis, major depression) often tell us little, sometimes almost nothing, about the actual problem, but a great deal about what we should think about it.

The prevalent diagnostic term "borderline personality disorder" provides a good example. In psychiatric literature the term has been used in a variety of ways, but for most professionals within psychiatry it refers to the idea that the problems of the patient are symptoms of a relatively deep-seated disturbance of the personality. It is commonly assumed that this disturbance has its origins in childhood, that it is difficult and time consuming to cure, and that it calls, if not for hospitalization, at least for long-term psychotherapeutic treatment.

All human problems can be "worded" in multiple ways. For instance, many alternative descriptions and definitions are available for the kind of problems that may become labeled within the psychiatric treatment system as "borderline disorder." The person could be simply said to be "having trouble" or to be "going through a turbulent period." Different "wordings" lead to significantly different ways of approaching problems (Efran & Heffner, 1991).

Depression is word commonly used to refer to situations where people see their life in a pessimistic light and suffer from a lack of energy for doing things. Many less disheartening expressions are available to characterize this kind of a problem. Common examples in English include "down in the dumps" and "feeling blue," but creative expressions such as "taking an inventory break" or "gathering energy" can be even more constructive.

The following example told by Ben provides an example of the use of creative naming in a case conventionally labeled as depression.

Brooding

One day when Tapani and I were writing together the phone rang. I picked up the receiver and on the line there was a woman who said she was visiting a workmate who was severely depressed and urgently needed an appointment with a psychiatrist. In the background I could hear the voice of a woman whining. The caller said that none of the several people who took turns visiting the woman knew what to do.

I asked to talk directly to the afflicted woman. With much effort the caller managed to get her to come to the phone. She explained that she had been absent from work for three weeks and that recently she had not even been able to get out of bed. I asked her if she had ever seen a psychiatrist and she said that because of a similar condition three years ago she had seen a psychiatrist, but the visit had been a disappointment. According to her, the psychiatrist had done nothing more than give her a prescription and tell her that all she could do was stay in bed and brood.

I asked her to hold on for a minute while I talked with my colleague. Tapani, who had been listening to the conversation through the speaker-phone, had picked up the word "brooding." With a twinkle in his eye he said, "Well, if she's broody, then obviously something is going to hatch sooner or later. At least that's what usually happens when hens brood. You could ask her about that."

I returned to the phone, "My colleague and I both noticed that you used the word 'brooding' to describe your condition. We got the idea that you are busy brooding something that needs to come out. A broody hen hatches chickens so we wondered what you might be hatching? We thought it might be an important decision you are about to make or something of that kind. How does that sound to you?"

"Yes, and I know what it is," she assured me.

"Please, don't tell me right now, but I am very interested to hear about it. Would you write and tell me? I promise to answer your letter."

We ended our conversation with this agreement.

After a few weeks she called me. Apologizing for not having written the promised letter she explained that she had recovered and that she was planning to return to work in the next week.

She also said that since our previous conversation she had made a major decision concerning her life. She worked on a boat and had for several years been involved with a man she worked with at sea while at the same time having a husband on shore. Some two years ago she had quit her double life by divorcing her husband, but to her lover's great disappointment she had not married him, nor had she even moved in with him. Conflicts resulted and the relationship between her and her lover had started to go badly. A few days before she called me she had decided to take the step of announcing that she was now willing to move in with her lover. Following this decision she had felt much better.

A person who drinks to excess does not have to be called an alcoholic. To build cooperation with such a person it may be more fruitful to use more benign expressions such as "excessive drinking" or "needing to cut back one's drinking." In some cases humorous alternatives may be appropriate; for example, one could suggest that the excessive drinker is "tormented by the booze-worm."

Chronic schizophrenia is the conventional label for long-lasting deviant behavior associated with bizarre ideas. This label, loaded with pessimistic overtones, can often be replaced with more down-to-earth descriptions, such as "in-the-corner lifestyle" (White, 1990). So-called psychotic symptoms can be worded as "peculiar thoughts," "daydreaming," "having ghosts," "being overly superstitious," or "being scared to death," depending on the nature of the actual problem.

The following example is a description of an interview we were invited to conduct in a child psychiatric hospital during our first trip to Leningrad. It illustrates how replacing biological psychiatric labels with ordinary phrases drawn from everyday language can empower people in their search for solutions. It is noteworthy that it is a global practice to label psychotic experiences as symptoms of a biological disturbance in the brain.

Wild Imagination

Juri, a 12-year-old boy, had been hospitalized recently because of peculiar ideas. He claimed to be seeing things and hearing voices. For example, he received messages from extraterrestrials every day and on one occasion he had seen a dragon in the toilet.

One of the psychiatrists at the hospital invited us to talk with Juri, who was also keen to talk to us. Juri proved to be alert and talkative. He readily answered all our questions, confirming that extraterrestrials talked to him almost constantly and explaining that the voices he heard had gradually become a nuisance to him.

Tapani told him, via the translator, "You might be interested to know, Juri, that there are children in our country who have problems just like yours. For example, I once met a boy who woke up in terror every night because creatures from another planet invaded his room. When I met the boy and his family, I told them that I suspected that these creatures actually wanted to play with the boy. However, since these creatures came from another planet, they did not know the difference between night and day, and therefore came at an inappropriate hour. We came up with the idea that on the following evening the boy would leave toys and comics lying on the floor so that when the creatures came they could play silently by themselves and not have to wake him up. This arrangement worked and the creatures stopped disturbing the boy."

Juri listened attentively to the translator and appeared to be very interested in the story. We then asked Juri if he had found any ways of stopping the voices from disturbing him. We said that we would be interested in carrying his solutions back home with us so that his practical ideas could be of benefit to other children with similar problems.

"I've found that it helps if I go to sleep during the day," said Juri.

"How interesting," we said and asked for more details, "Is it important to actually sleep or is it enough just to lie down and relax?"

"No, it isn't enough," explained Juri in a very matter-of-fact tone. "You really must sleep."

"For how long?" we asked.

"Two hours," said Juri.

We thanked Juri for his information. Tapani explained that in his experience extraterrestrials begin to bother people when they have important guidance to offer that person.

"When they become convinced that you have learned what they want to teach you, they usually go away and leave you alone," said Tapani.

Juri agreed with this and said, "I already know what it is they want to teach me."

"It's very good that you know, but you don't need to tell us about it right now. Talk about it later with your doctor."

Juri agreed, we thanked each other, and he was taken back to his ward by a nurse.

We then talked about Juri with his psychiatrist. He explained to us that Juri's symptoms indicated childhood schizophrenia and that he had planned to put him on antipsychotic medication.

Ben said bluntly, "We prefer to call these kinds of problems 'wild imagination.'"

"I understand you," said the psychiatrist, "but how can we tell whether this is schizophrenia or wild imagination? I agree that your approach can be used to treat wild imagination but schizophrenia requires medication."

"You're right," said Ben more tactfully. "The question of differential diagnosis is very important; it is sometimes difficult to distinguish between the two. We usually start from the assumption that these kinds of problems are caused by wild imagination and try to solve them by using imagination techniques. Only after failing to bring about positive results with this approach do we consider the diagnosis of schizophrenia."

The psychiatrist accepted this approach to the dilemma of differential diagnosis and the meeting was closed. We heard later from the psychologist who had arranged our visit to the hospital that after our visit Juri had been diagnosed as having "letutshia fantazia" (flying imagination). He had not been put on medication and his treatment had taken the form we had suggested. He had been discharged some two weeks after our visit.

Many psychological terms and expressions, let alone diagnostic labels in psychiatric classification systems such as the DSM-III-R, suggest that problems are deep seated, persistent, or hard to cure. A good proportion of frequently heard terms, such as "weak ego," "hyperactivity," "psychopath," "antisocial personality," "dependent personality," "alcoholic," "drug-addict," "neurotic," "schizophrenic," "manic-depressive," "autistic," "low self-esteem," "narcissism," "symbiosis," belong to this category. Baruch Shulem, a therapist from Jerusalem, has mockingly remarked that the acronym DSM appears to stand for the "Dark Side of Man"; he has proposed that the DSM should be replaced by the BSM where the letters stand for "Bright Side of Man" (Schulem 1988).

The label "weak ego" or "ego weakness," frequently used in child psychiatry at least in our own country, is an illustration of a diagnostic label which indicates that a child's problems are severe and persistent. On one occasion this concept came up when Ben was lecturing to a group of special teachers about using creativity when helping to solve children's problems. Towards the end of the lecture one of the participants said, "What you say seems quite reasonable to me, but what do you do in cases where the child has such a weak ego that it's as leaky as a sieve?" She went on to explain, "I work presently with a boy who is shy and who lacks all initiative. I once asked each of my pupils to draw a picture of the animal which they felt represented them best. This boy drew a picture of a tiger–which is the exact opposite of what he actually is."

This led to a discussion of the meaning of the tiger. It emerged that the tiger could be interpreted either as an image of what the boy would like to be but knows that he is not or as a symbol of the boy's true self. According to the latter view, there was in fact a dormant tiger slumbering inside the boy even if, for one reason or another, he had chosen not to let it show.

Since then the metaphor of the dormant tiger has served us as a reminder of the importance of using language which emphasizes people's resources rather than their failings.

Related to the notion of "ego weakness" is the concept "early disturbance." This diagnostic term has emerged from within psychodynamic child psychiatry. It has been widely applied in some places, not only within the helping professions but even within the educational system.

"Early disturbance" refers to the psychoanalytic notion that problems have their origin in infancy, more specifically in the early relationship between the child and its caretaker, usually mother. By implication, the concept implies blame on the mother and suggests that the problems are deep-seated.

When clients or professionals are talking about problems using such weighty labels as "early disturbance" or "ego weakness," it may prove useful to propose the substitution of such terms with less pathologizing ones. However, challenging or abandoning expert diagnostic terms is not easy. We have found that in such instances humor is frequently more successful than trying to be reasonable. Instead of saying "I don't think it's useful to say that this child has an early disturbance," it may be more fruitful to say, "That's good because people with such a diagnosis are particularly good at solving their problems," or perhaps, "That makes two of us!"

The acronym MBD (Minimal Brain Dysfunction) has become a widespread diagnosis in several European countries in a similar fashion to ADD (Attention Deficit Disorder) in the United States. MBD was introduced by medical experts to refer to children exhibiting multiple soft neurological signs, e.g., clumsiness, lack of coordination, learning difficulties, distractibility, and marginal deviations in EEG. Children with such problems often manifested behavioral problems, such as impulsivity or aggressive behavior. Gradually MBD became a popular diagnosis. It has been attached by medical experts to legion children with behavior problems, even when there has been little reason to suspect an underlying neurological dysfunction.

There are benefits in situations where a child's behavioral problem is seen as symptomatic of MBD — or any other brain defect such as mental retardation. Such a view can help to dissolve blame and guilt and may also encourage adults to be

more patient with the child. The drawback of attributing undesirable behavior to brain dysfunction is that it often impedes
the search for solutions. When parents and teachers are led to
believe that a child's behavioral problem is caused by an underlying brain defect, they often become demoralized and lose
their natural tendency to seek solutions. For example, Tapani
once met a father who was totally unable to control his 8-year-
old boy who had been diagnosed as having MBD. When the
father was asked what he would do if the boy didn't actually
have MBD, he said that he would behave as he did towards his
elder son. When asked how he had managed to control the elder
son, he said, "I simply grabbed hold of him and held him in my
lap until he calmed down."

We have found that instead of challenging the correctness of
a previously attached diagnosis of MBD, it is often more useful
to help people change their way of thinking about MBD. For
this purpose we have coined a new term, MBC. This acronym
refers to "Maximal Brain Capacity" – something which exists in
all children with "Minimal Brain Dysfunction."

Many diagnostic terms presuppose the existence of an underlying disorder which is held responsible for the person's presenting problems. This is particularly true for terms that include the idea of latency, such as "latent homosexuality," "latent
schizophrenia," "masked depression," "pent-up aggression," "unresolved grief," etc.

The presupposition that people have latent or dormant problems may unfortunately become self-verifying. For example, a
medical doctor assumes that a patient's problems are symptomatic of "masked depression." In order to verify his hypothesis the doctor will ask questions about hardships in the patient's life. As the conversation becomes increasingly focused
on troubles, the patient becomes sorrowful. This quite appropriate reaction to the doctor's questioning can then be interpreted as evidence confirming the original hypothesis.

Fortunately, the attribution of dormant positive qualities is
also self-fulfilling. A colleague or ours, Eero Riikonen, once
coined the playful term "latent joy." This novel diagnostic cate-

gory has proved very useful in helping people focus on their potential rather than on their problems.

In the following example Tapani suggests to the client that she is suffering from "latent joy."

Latent Joy

Maria requested a consultation because of feelings of emptiness and depression. When she came she told me about her circumstances in order to help me understand her current hopelessness. She explained that she was employed as a designer in a large garment company. The whole garment industry was presently in a crisis and numerous companies were collapsing. Employees in the industry, designers in particular, lived under almost intolerable pressure.

In addition to learning about Maria's work related problems, I also heard about her various marital difficulties. I then asked about her hopes for the future. She said, among other things, that she had for years aspired to devote more time to painting.

I observed that Maria was dressed all in black and asked her about it, "How long have you been wearing black?"

"I have been wearing black clothes at work for as long as I can remember," she said.

"The color of your clothing seems to reflect the way you feel, doesn't it?" I said.

"Yes, it does, but I don't mean it that way. Most designers wear black," she explained.

"You know, when I look at your appearance it reflects your mood, but if I listen to the way you talk I hear a quite different feeling. I sense that deep down you are a joyful person. Could it be that your joy is simply dormant, as if you were suffering from what one of my colleagues calls 'latent joy'?"

"Maybe . . . I used to be a cheerful person."

"There's a way to find out. You could begin to wear more colorful clothes and see what happens. How about it?" I asked.

"No, I like to wear black. It's my style," she objected.

"I see . . . and do you also wear black underwear?" I asked.

"As a matter of fact, I do," she confessed.

"In that case you could change to bright-colored underwear without anybody noticing anything. After all, people don't notice your latent joy either."

I saw Maria four more times over a period of half a year. Twelve months after the final session I received an invitation to an art gallery. Along with the card was a note, "You are welcome to my exhibition to choose a painting for yourself, not as a fee for your services, but as a memento, because I believe I have at last found my latent joy."

Ben was once invited to talk to the staff of a psychiatric inpatient unit on how to improve collaboration with patients' families. He explained to the staff that many psychiatric labels imply that problems lie within the family, thus putting successful collaboration at stake. After an evaluation of the drawbacks of using the diagnosis of "borderline personality disorder," Ben asked the group what was the most frequent diagnosis used on their ward. It emerged that it was "a crisis of becoming independent."

Ben asked about the explanation behind patients' difficulties in becoming independent from their families. It turned out that the common explanation was that patients' parents interfered with their natural growth. Quite commonly, the patient's mother was considered to be overly protective or excessively involved.

"All right, if most of our terms imply blame, is there an alternative? What terms should we then use for these problems?" asked someone in the group.

"I honestly don't know," said Ben and asked the group for help.

After a pause one of the nurses said, "Perhaps we could speak of 'a quest' or 'the search for a life direction'." His suggestions were received favorably.

Fortunately, therapists do not carry the sole responsibility for finding constructive words and expressions for problems; clients themselves often come up with excellent suggestions. For example, we once interviewed a couple who had suffered a two-year period of turmoil in their marriage. When asked what "nickname" they might use in the future to refer to this turbulent phase in their life, they discussed this together for a while and then decided to call it "the guerilla period." We mildly protested by reminding them that the word "guerilla" was associated with warfare, but the spouses held onto their selection. After the session we learned from their therapist that these people were former political activists for whom the word "guerilla" had positive associations – revolution and progress.

We have illustrated in this chapter that terminology suggestive of pathology can have a variety of unfortunate consequences. One should bear in mind, however, that people may not be as vulnerable to our words as we might expect. This fact was brought home to us on the streets of Budapest when we attended a European family therapy conference there. A group of conference participants decided to visit a rock club one evening in order to hear a local band playing. When we arrived at the club we found to our disappointment that it was closed. Outside the entrance we made contact with a young Hungarian couple, who had also come there in vain. They invited us to accompany them to another club and we readily accepted the invitation.

As we were walking along the young man, who spoke English, told us that he was a musician and that he had just returned from a European tour. Ben explained that we were a group of psychiatrists, psychologists, social workers and other professionals from different countries and that we were in Budapest for a conference on psychotherapy. The young man showed interest and related his own experience. He said that some time ago he had undergone psychiatric treatment and that the doctors had come to the conclusion that he had a borderline personality disorder. Ben, who is an ardent opponent of the diagnosis said, "Oh, I don't believe you are borderline. In fact, the whole concept is disputable, and many people in our field don't believe in it at all." The man pondered for a while then shrugged his shoulders and said understandingly, "Well, psychiatry is still a young discipline."

5

FRUITFUL EXPLANATIONS

Petri, who was a first-grader in school, had become known as a menace at the afternoon care center he attended every day after school. He had a terrible habit of not only constantly teasing smaller children but also hitting them. The staff at the care center felt helpless in the face of this problem. They demanded that Petri be transferred to another care center specializing in care of disturbed children. The staff notified the local child guidance clinic where Sinikka, a social worker who was a participant in our training group, established contact with the family. After having met the family a number of times without any significant progress, Sinikka decided to invite the family in for a consultation session with us.

The session started with Sinikka making an introduction. She acquainted the training group with the members of the family and then briefly explained the problem. We then opened the discussion by asking Sinikka what she believed was the cause of the problem. She explained that for the past year mother had worked so hard that she had not had the time and energy to give Petri the amount of attention that he needed.

This conventional explanation had, however, not served to solve the problem and we suspected that mother would not feel comfortable with it.

However, when we asked mother what she thought the cause of the problem was, we found that she agreed with

Sinikka. She began to speak about how she often worked extra hours and for that reason was so worn out in the evenings that she didn't have enough patience with her children. She also said that she had come to the conclusion that she needed to reduce the amount of extra hours worked even if it meant possibly jeopardizing her career development.

We next turned to Petri, who had been listening attentively to the discussion, as children usually do if the conversation is carried out so that they can understand what is said. "What do you say, Petri? Do you hit the other children because your mom does not have enough time for you?"

Petri seemed perplexed and all he could say was, "How can it be mother's fault if I hit other children?"

"Then whose fault is it?" we asked.

"It's my own fault," he said.

"And in that case what should be done about it?"

"I should be punished."

"And who should be the one to punish you?"

"Mom," said Petri in his businesslike manner.

"Then how should you be punished?"

"I should be hit as hard as I hit the others."

"But that's against the law," we objected. "It doesn't matter," said Petri.

"Yes it does," we argued kindly, "the child protection people can come and scold your mother if they find out that she is trying to solve the problem by spanking you."

"I will explain to them if they come," said Petri in such a sweet way that the group could not help laughing.

We then asked Sinikka and the mother if they would be willing to drop the idea that Petri's problems were caused by the mother.

"Would you be willing to consider the possibility that the two problems — Petri's hitting at the care center and mother's working so much and being tired at home — are unrelated?"

This view was welcomed by both mother and Sinikka.

We then divided the training group into smaller, teams each of which had the task of coming up with recommendations about what should be done to solve the problem. After about a quarter of an hour the teams came together again to discuss their suggestions. The conversation led to the agreement that Sinikka, mother, and Petri should together speak with the two teachers at the day care center. They should then explain to the teachers that Petri had himself declared that punishment would be the best way to stop him from doing what he did. It was suggested that traditional punishment should be replaced by some form of atonement, where Petri would have to do something good in reparation for the bad he had done. This suggestion was accepted by everyone. Sinikka noted that the teachers at the day care were very nice people and likely to cooperate. We ended the session and wished them good luck in their venture. Later on we heard from Sinikka that the planned meeting had been arranged and that it had led to a successful resolution of the problem.

When working in a solution-oriented manner the focus of therapeutic conversations is predominantly forward-looking, and explaining and interpreting problems merit little or no attention at all. In reality, however, some degree of explanation is inevitable. Clients wonder about the causes of their problems, and professionals, even when they deliberately ignore the subject, cannot avoid conveying some of their ideas about the origin of clients' problems. Our choice of words, the questions we ask, and the actions we recommend always contain some elements of explanation.

Explanations of problems determine to a great degree what we believe needs to be done to solve them. For example, explaining a child's problem in terms of family dysfunction directs the therapist to try and do something about the alleged dysfunction, just as when people in other cultures believe that a problem is caused by an angered ancestor they try to find a way to placate that ancestor.

The way we explain problems and the actions we take to

solve them are tightly interconnected. It is not only that a particular explanation leads to certain kinds of solutions, but also that particular solutions reflect certain types of explanations. A change in the way we explain a problem tends to result in a change in the way in which we attempt to solve it and vice versa.

Explanations differ in the extent to which they attribute blame and elicit shame. Therefore some explanations are better than others in fostering collaboration and creativity. When it appears that current explanations impede finding solutions, the replacement of those explanations with new ones can be useful.

There are multiple ways of explaining a particular piece of behavior. For example, if a father does not join a family therapy session despite a specific invitation, his behavior may be accounted for in a variety of ways. It may be thought that his absence is caused by a lack of caring for his family, that he is afraid of being condemned by professionals, or that he is truly too busy to attend the session. Different explanations evoke different emotional and behavioral responses; some of these responses are more likely than others to enhance collaboration and thus contribute to the emergence of solutions.

In the following example, drawn from our ongoing seminar, a mother who was enraged with her daughter was offered a new explanation to account for the daughter's recent behavior. This alternative explanation enabled the mother to become more sympathetic toward her daughter.

The Teenage Social Worker

Silja had recently encountered insurmountable problems with her 16-year-old daughter, Nina. Nina had suffered from diabetes since early childhood but she had never had any other problems. Since Nina started dating an 18-year-old boy, Rick, a few months previously there had been a drastic change in her behavior. Silja did not approve of Rick, who had problems with his parents, did not go to school, and had no job. Silja suspected that he was involved with drugs.

One evening, just a few weeks earlier, Nina and Rick were caressing each other in Nina's room and it was getting late. Silja interrupted them and said that it was time for Rick to leave. Rick informed Silja that he intended to stay the night. The ensuing argument resulted in Nina's packing her bag and disappearing into the night with Rick.

This incident upset Silja profoundly, not only because she had no idea where the youngsters had gone but also because she was very concerned that Nina might not take proper care of her diabetes.

A couple of days later Silja spoke on the phone with Rick's parents, who claimed that they knew nothing about Nina's whereabouts. Unconvinced, Silja called the police who called at Rick's house. They found Nina there and brought her home, but the next day she was back with Rick's family again. Silja insisted that Nina come home immediately, but she refused. The whole affair was an enormous blow to Silja who, understandably, was enraged not only at her daughter but also at Rick and his parents.

After having heard Silja's description of the situation, we explained to her that Nina was in a corner. As long as Silja was critical of Rick, Nina had no choice but to defend him.

Silja said, "I understand that, but don't tell me that I must become friendly with Rick and his folks." It appeared to be impossible for her to consider taking a conciliatory stance towards these people whom she felt had betrayed her.

We decided to offer Silja a more positive way of looking at her daughter's recent behavior. Tapani said, "Tell me, does your daughter have a big heart? . . . Does she care for others and like to help people with their problems?"

"Yes, she's always been that way. She is a very caring girl, that's why I can't understand her behaving this way."

Tapani continued, "I understand that Rick has had a number of problems?"

"Yes, that's right. His parents even kicked him out some time ago," confirmed Silja.

"You know, I've noticed that sometimes girls of a certain age find someone who has problems and devote themselves completely to helping that person," said Tapani. "Could it be that this is what has happened with Nina? Has she, perhaps, taken Rick under her wing?"

Ben offered support for this new explanation, "Nina, who seems to be well liked by Rick's parents, has actually succeeded in helping Rick by improving his relationship with his parents, hasn't she?"

"That's true. Also, according to his parents, both Nina and Rick are presently attending school. So maybe she actually is taking care of him," said Silja.

"Perhaps when teenagers take the role of 'social worker' they commit themselves so profoundly that they put the mission before their family," said Ben.

"And your daughter probably knows that guys come and go but mothers stay forever," continued Tapani.

We recommended to Silja that she discuss the situation with Nina along this new line. She accepted the suggestion and we ended the session.

A month later we heard more about the case from the friend of Silja's who had originally invited her for consultation. She told us that a few days after the session Silja had spoken on the phone with Nina. She had followed our recommendations and told Nina that up until now she had not understood how much it meant for Nina to help Rick. After this conversation the ice had melted. When Silja returned home from work the next day Nina had been at home. She had prepared a pot of hot coffee and sandwiches for Silja and left a friendly note. This gesture was the beginning of a reunion between mother and daughter. Soon Nina had moved back home and Silja was no longer worried about the situation, even though Nina continued to see Rick.

In order for explanations to be helpful they do not necessarily have to appear conventional or sensible. Uncommon, imaginative explanations are often excellent catalysts for finding solutions.

In the following example Tapani suggests an imaginative explanation in order to help one of our group members find a new way of dealing with a persistent marital conflict.

The Cupboard Door

One of our trainees explained that she and her husband argued almost daily about a certain cupboard door. She had the habit of leaving the door open and the open door irritated him. When he started complaining, she countered and the exchange soon escalated into a full-blown row.

I asked her whether she wanted to learn to remember to close the door behind her or to get her husband to stop complaining. She explained that the whole problem was caused by her husband's rigid orderliness, a characteristic which (according to her) ran in his family. She expected us to offer ideas about how she could change him.

After we had discussed her situation in the group for a while I suggested that she tell her husband that she had discussed her habit of leaving the cupboard door open with her training group which includes many experienced psychologists. She should say that according to the group her leaving the cupboard door open was actually a "subconscious" or perhaps even "preconscious" symbolic gesture signifying her readiness to have sex with her husband. For a moment she was startled by this far-fetched explanation, but having an open mind she begun to laugh and accepted the task.

When the same group met again two weeks later, the trainee told us that there had been no arguments at all between her and her husband concerning the cupboard door once she had given him the suggested explanation.

We were all curious to know what had happened, "Well, what did your husband say?" we asked.

"He said it was the craziest thing he had ever heard."

"And . . . ?"

"Well, since then, whenever I've left the door open he hasn't said anything at all. He just closes the door himself." We all laughed.

The following story provided by Ben is another illustration of the use of creative explanations involving sexual overtones.

Highly Potent

I was once part of a panel on a phone-in radio talk show with four other mental health professionals. We were answering listeners' questions about fears and phobias. One of the callers was a young man who said that he suffered from what he called "coffee-cup neurosis," a pertinent lay term for what is called in psychiatry "social phobia," a common problem which often includes trembling of the hands when a person is drinking coffee in company. After the other professionals had offered their matter-of-fact explanations and suggestions, Ben said, tongue in cheek, "According to the latest research there is evidence that this problem is related to a high level of sexual potency." There was a few seconds' silence before the caller released a hesitant chuckle. "This is not a laughing matter," continued Ben. "In the United States many people are already seeking therapy because they are worried about their coffee-cup neurosis fading away."

This explanation to account for "coffee-cup neurosis" amused the caller and during the brief discussion the panel had in the studio after the show it was agreed that there is room for more humor in the field of mental health.

In the following case Ben shows that the use of creative explanations is not limited to minor difficulties but that they can also be built upon when working with major problems. In this case the family is proposed a positive explanation for the daughter's suicide attempt.

A Dangerous Way to Teach Philosophy

I was working with a group of physicians at a hospital. One morning I was asked to interview Sini, a 17-year-old girl who was accompanied by her parents.

Sini had attempted to commit suicide a few days earlier by taking an overdose of tranquilizers. After hearing what had occurred, I asked the parents why they thought Sini had taken the overdose in order to find out whether they considered that they were to blame.

The parents offered explanations in which they blamed themselves for what had happened. They said, for example, "We haven't paid enough attention to her," "we've overlooked her difficulties," and "we've failed to take her problems seriously." I then turned to Sini who, judging from her expression, didn't seem to agree with her parents. I asked her for her own explanation, but she didn't give an answer.

I accepted her response and said, "It might be a good idea to keep your explanation to yourself for the time being." I then continued, "Sini, I have a hunch about why you did it. Would you like to hear it?"

"Yes," said Sini.

"I get the feeling that you are quite a philosophical person. I mean that you like to think about the meaning of life and things of that sort. Am I right?"

Sini smiled and seemed pleased with my characterization of her. Her parents confirmed that I was correct. They said that Sini enjoyed poetry and took pleasure in reading non-fiction literature.

I continued, "My explanation for your suicide attempt is, that for one reason or another, you wanted to teach your parents something valuable and important about life, something you had begun to understand and that you wanted to convey to them. That's not such a bad idea . . . I

mean, for children to teach their parents about the philosophy of life. But the way in which you chose to do the
teaching was certainly not the best possible one. It could
have cost you your life."

The parents approved of this explanation of mine and,
judging from Sini's nonverbal communication, she
seemed to like it, too.

"You know, Sini," I suggested, "you could find a safer
way of teaching your parents about the philosophy of life.
Why don't you write a fairy tale for your parents, a story
which portrays, in a symbolic way, the things about life
that you want to teach your parents. That way you can
teach them without having to harm yourself. How about
it?"

"I don't know. I'm not very good at writing fairy tales,"
said Sini.

"All right," I continued. "It doesn't necessarily have to
be a fairy tale. It could be a story, a poem, or even a
collection of quotations or words of wisdom. It could be
anything that tells them in a metaphorical way whatever
it is you want to teach them. How does that sound?"

"I can try," said Sini. "I could write something."

"Good, and could you make photocopies of the writing?" I asked.

"I can do that at work," said father.

"That's good, since my suggestion is that you make a
few copies of what Sini writes so that you and mother can
each have your own copy to study and you can bring a
copy to us as well."

I turned to the parents and said, "When you get your
copy, read it carefully and try to get an idea of what it is
that Sini wants to teach you about life. Keep your conclusions to yourselves and when we meet again we'll talk
about it more."

In the follow-up session a few weeks later all members
of the family looked much brighter. Sini had recovered
well and was now back in school. Father handed me a
sheet of paper on which there were some ten passages of

wisdom. There were pieces of limericks from popular songs, some clever rhymes she had invented herself, and a few more serious words of wisdom. Here are some examples:

- The world changes as you mature – how very interesting.
- One's clothes often fit too well, there should be meters of space for growth.
- Love your fellow as you love yourself.
- "Whiz" said life and disappeared, "poof" said the behind and smelled.
- It is upsetting to realize how unbearable people can be, but most upsetting of all is to realize that one's own self is only human.
- Sometimes it feels as if one is part of a complex mathematical equation which can take a myriad of forms, but where the end result is always the same.

I turned to the parents and asked what they had made of these quotations. It emerged that they had not read the phrases as teachings, but as veiled criticism of themselves.

I felt the need to explain, "The idea is not to find out what Sini's quotations say about you, but to discover what they reveal about her philosophy of life."

We took a break while the family had coffee. During the break I discussed the meaning of Sini's quotations with the rest of our group, who had observed the session through a one-way mirror.

When the family returned I gave them a summary of my discussion with the group. I said that we had analyzed Sini's quotations and asked them whether they were interested in hearing our conclusions. They were quite keen to learn of our interpretations.

"We found Sini's quotations interesting and amusing," I said. "They reflect a sense of optimism and growth, realization of the finality of life, and a wonderful sense of humor, which I personally believe to be one of life's great gifts."

Our comments seemed to give Sini and her parents a lift. We ended the session without agreeing on any further family meetings.

I called the family half a year after the second session and spoke with the father. He said that, although they had all been pleased with the two sessions, at the time he and his wife would have wanted to return for a few more sessions if it would have been possible. Sini, however, had recovered well from her crisis and was presently working abroad.

When helping children to solve problems, imaginary explanations involving fairies, monsters, goblins, trolls, or gremlins are not only enticing but also effective. To help families where a child is suffering from soiling, Michael White has proposed a charming approach (White, 1984). The therapist explains to the family that the problem is caused by a nasty little creature known by the name of Sneaky Poo. It is neither the child nor the parents who are responsible for the problem but Sneaky Poo. Based on this idea a program is devised where the whole family cooperates to conquer Sneaky Poo. This game-like program includes running competitions with Sneaky Poo, scaring Sneaky Poo with pictures of tigers, sitting on the toilet for ten minutes after meals, etc. A comparable approach has also been used with children suffering from bed-wetting, in other words, helping children to escape the tricks of Sneaky Pee.

Using fantasy creatures as scapegoats has a number of benefits. These include easing the discussion of problems, increasing collaboration, and introducing a degree of playfulness, which inspires people to come up with creative solutions. The following example, provided by Ben, illustrates these points.

The Snatcher

Milli was a seven-year-old girl who had developed the habit of stealing money from the members of her family. She had started by stealing money from her parents' pockets, but recently she had begun to take it from wherever she could find it. On several occasions she had emptied her big brother's wallet and even her grandmother was no longer safe. She had also enticed her friend into becoming her accomplice. The two girls had stolen a fifty mark note (about $15) from her friend's mother's purse. The girls had then gone to their local kiosk to spend the whole sum on sweets. The kiosk owner had become suspicious and had refused to allow them to spend more than half the money. They then hid the rest of the money in the garden. The parents had threatened Milli with corporal punishment to make her reveal the hiding place. Mother and Milli had been visiting the child guidance center regularly for two months, but there had been no improvement.

Both mother and the therapists at the child guidance center had assumed that the problem was caused by sibling jealousy. This idea was based on the fact that the stealing had started soon after the birth of Milli's baby sister. Milli did not appear to agree with this explanation; whenever she was asked to explain why she stole money she answered, "I don't know."

I turned to Milli who was drawing and said, "I think I know what it is that's causing you to take money from other people's pockets and wallets. It's the Snatcher-Monster. I know that Snatcher-Monster," I said and then whispered into Milli's ear as if I was the Monster, "He says, 'Snatch the money, snatch the money, we'll buy lots of sweets; snatch the money, snatch the money, we'll buy lots of sweets.'"

Milli immediately caught the idea of the Snatcher-Monster. She smiled and started to draw a picture of him. I said that it was possible to send the Snatcher-Monster packing, but that he was so cunning that we would have to find a clever way to fool him. I suggested that we split into two groups to devise possible strategies for dealing with the Monster. I joined mother and the therapist in an adjacent room while the rest of the supervision group stayed and talked with Milli.

I asked mother what she thought about the idea of

blaming the Snatcher-Monster. She said she liked it and thought it could be useful. When I asked her what she thought her husband might think, she replied that as he had a good sense of humor he would certainly like the idea. We devised the following plan with mother: She was to obtain a few wallets and place in each of them a low value foreign currency banknote. She was to carefully hide the wallets around the house and then invite Milli to try and find them. For every foreign note that Milli found mother would give her one mark (about a quarter) to be spent in any way she liked. The purpose of this game was to help Milli thumb her nose at the Snatcher-Monster by offering her a legitimate way of obtaining extra money when she found a wallet.

We rejoined the others and found that Milli had completed her drawing of the horrible looking Snatcher-Monster. We admired his scary appearance. I explained to Milli that mother and I had devised a plan to send the monster packing and that she would find out about it very soon. We ended the session.

Two months later I learned that the stealing appeared to have stopped after our session and mother had felt that there had been no need to carry out the game of the hidden wallets. The therapists had asked Milli how she had done it. She had answered cutely, "I won't tell."

Upon hearing that Milli had overcome her problem I decided to send her a postcard to congratulate her. I looked through my daughter's selection of postcards and chose a charming card which had a picture of a sweet little puppy. I wrote the following message on the card, "Congratulations on sending the Snatcher-Monster packing," and signed it, "All the best from Uncle Ben." (The therapist had told me that Uncle Ben was what Milli had called me.)

Soon after I sent the card my eight-year-old daughter discovered that without her permission I had taken her best ever puppy postcard. She was justifiably angry with me. As I apologized and promised to replace the card I realized who the Snatcher-Monster had chosen as his next victim!

Using imaginary explanations comes naturally when working with children but such an approach is also applicable to adults, as the following example shows.

The Muiluttaja

We were asked to instruct a newly formed group of volunteers who had the task of giving support to ex-addicts enrolled in a two-year residential recovery program at a rural institution.

Instead of offering traditional supervision to the volunteers, we proposed that a get-together be arranged to discuss what was expected of them. This meeting was to be an opportunity for the ex-users, their families, staff, and volunteers to mutually discuss and agree on the role of the "supporters" in the overall treatment plan.

Our proposal was accepted and a two-day workshop was arranged at the residential treatment home. All the 40 people present sat in a large circle, and after they had introduced themselves we opened a discussion about the perennial question of why young people use drugs. We justified this topic by claiming that different views about the causes of abuse would lead to different ideas about what should be expected from the volunteers. The group proposed some dozen prevalent explanations, including genetic predisposition, difficult childhood, emotional disturbance, bad company, and the addictive effect of the drugs. After all the explanations had been presented there was a gloomy atmosphere in the room. We then announced, quite seriously, that none of these explanations was correct. The true cause of drug abuse, we proclaimed, was a nasty creature called "The Muiluttaja."

We had coined the term "Muiluttaja" just a few minutes earlier during the coffee break. The root of the word is

derived from the Finnish word "muilutus," which originally refers to unexpected forcible transportation and ejec-
tion of people during the interwar period by the fascists.
These transportations were used as a form of intimidation
and they frequently involved the use of violence.

The word "Muiluttaja" therefore effectively personifies
oppression and tyranny. This unconventional explanation, which put the blame on an imaginary being rather
than any of the people present, was well received.

We then divided into smaller discussion groups and
gave each of them the task of listing the Muiluttaja's likes
and dislikes. Among other things it turned out that the
Muiluttaja liked bad feelings, isolation from others, and
any discussion centering on drugs. As well as taking particular pleasure in hearing people blame one another, the
Muiluttaja disliked work, future plans, socializing with
normal people, caring for the well-being of others, etc.

Having identified the Muiluttaja's likes and dislikes,
we set out in small groups to devise a plan for getting rid
of it. This produced a host of excellent ideas, the most well
received being a suggestion that the staff, the ex-users,
the families, and the volunteers would jointly set up an
association with the name "The Anti-Muiluttaja Association" or AMA. The goal of the association was to get rid of
the Muiluttaja through organizing meetings and carrying
out joint ventures.

The first joint venture was to organize an informal "get-
to-know-each-other" weekend for volunteers, recovering
ex-users and parents. The weekend was held within the
next month and it turned out successfully. It became the
first event of a regular series of get-togethers and weekend trips subsequently arranged by the group.

The volunteers, who had originally been invited to become psychological "supporters," are now viewed as
"friends." They see their main function to be that of helping ex-users make contact with people who are not involved with drugs in any way. The project has been successful, particularly in terms of including families in the

recovery process and improving collaboration between the various groups involved.

Sometimes clients' own explanations for their problems may appear inappropriate to professionals. In such cases therapists often try to persuade the client to adopt another explanation. For example, if the parents of a boy presume that his behavioral problems are caused by the fact that he struck his head as an infant, the therapist may wish the parents to adopt another explanation in order for them to become empowered to solve the problem.

Sometimes when clients are convinced beyond doubt of the correctness of their own explanation, it may prove futile to try and persuade them otherwise. In such situations the therapist may choose to subscribe to the principle of "don't argue with the client" and accept the client's explanation at face value.

The following story, provided by Tapani, dates back to his early years as a brief therapist. It illustrates the principle of accepting clients' explanations and deducing a relevant solution.

The Bead Test

Seventeen-year-old Anni was in serious trouble. She was referred to me by an adolescent psychiatric ward from which she had been discharged for bringing drugs onto the premises. When I first saw her she was suicidal and psychotic. At our first session I managed to get her to agree to bring me her entire collection of tranquilizers and razor blades. We agreed that should she become beset by an urge to take her life she was to consult me before harming herself, as her suicide "utensils" were now in my possession. This agreement was very helpful, even though it did not eliminate her suicidal impulses at once. Early in the following three years of therapy Anni brought up her most pressing problem.

"I have sinned," she said, "and I am therefore being punished. On many nights Satan has appeared to me in the form of a man. He says that he will come and kill me."

I was puzzled by this bizarre idea and asked her how Satan would be able to do that. She explained that he would kill her by touching and that his touch would doom her to eternal damnation. I came to think of an old story I once heard Paul Watzlawick relate at a conference. The oriental tale tells of a man who is instructed to perform a test in order to find out whether the spirits that are harassing him should be ignored or taken seriously. Taking my line from that story, I suggested that Anni carry out an experiment to determine whether or not her Satan was really powerful enough to kill.

I said, "Here at our clinic we used to have a social worker who spent several years in Brazil. He told us that there are lots of people in Brazil who are harassed by demons. He also said that according to the Brazilians not all demons are alike. Some are genuinely dangerous but others are simply cheating. The cheating ones manage to create an illusion of power. Such demons are, however, just liars. There is a test you could do to find out whether your Satan is just one of those liars."

Anni showed interest in doing the test so I gave her the following instructions. She was to buy one small plastic bag of red beads and another of black beads. Next time Satan appeared she was to seize a random number of both red and black beads and conceal them in her fist. She was then to ask Satan how many red beads and how many black beads there were in her hand. If Satan was unable to tell it would be a sure sign that he was just one of those liars. Anni accepted the idea and said she would try it out.

At the next session Anni reported that when Satan had appeared and threatened to touch her she had picked up an unknown number of both red and black beads. She had then asked the Satan how many black beads she had in her hand. Satan had said 16. When Anni counted the beads in her hand there were exactly 16 black ones. She asked me how I could explain that.

At first I was taken aback. I feared I had painted myself into a corner and only managed to perpetuate the problem. I said, "How about the red beads? Did Satan know their number as well?"

"No he didn't," Anni replied. "He said there were 14 beads but there were only nine . . . but how do you explain the fact that he knew the exact number of black beads?" she persisted.

I thought for a while and finally said, "He probably guessed it; everybody guesses right sometimes."

Anni smiled and accepted my answer. After this she hardly ever mentioned Satan again and apparently her tormentor faded away. For many years I hesitated to tell my colleagues about the unorthodox way in which Anni and I dealt with her Satan.

All therapists are familiar with the experience of offering an idea to a person who does not seem at all interested in accepting it. In one of our training groups some of the participants were particularly eager to persuade clients to accept their ideas, even when those clients clearly indicated that they disagreed. We named such behavior "pushing" and discussed the drawbacks; the group then agreed to abstain from doing it. Pushing, however, continued to take place so we thought of another solution. The group composed a simple melody for the words "push, push, push" and decided to gently sing the song when pushing occurred in sessions. The song was actually used a few times with favorable results.

It is important to be gentle when suggesting new explanations to clients. Rather than instructing people what to think about the cause of their problem, it is better to tell them a story that portrays the idea or to invite them to become a partner in the search for fruitful explanations. Bringing out several alternative explanations rather than suggesting only one reminds clients (as well as ourselves) about the importance of keeping an open mind.

Stories from one's own life, from cases one has seen, or from literature offer a sensitive way of proposing new ways of thinking to clients. We have used many of the stories told in this book to make a point. Stories leave the door open for clients to decide for themselves whether to accept or reject the various explanations embedded in the story.

Explanations can be examined, not in terms of whether they are correct or not but in terms of what actions they invoke. This allows for new solutions to emerge without the need for clients to approve of those explanations. Proposals can take the form, "Suppose your problem were indeed caused by so and so, what would you do in that case?" For example, a therapist might ask a couple suffering from intense marital discord, "Someone might say that deep down your problem stems from your intense and secret passion for each other. Let's suppose that this is indeed the real cause of your problem – what then needs to be done to solve it?"

In this chapter we have discussed the generation of alternative explanations from the point of view of the therapist. It should be emphasized, however, that if clients are exposed to the principle of looking for fruitful explanations they often become quite keen in discovering alternative explanations by themselves. Specific questions, such as "How would people explain this problem in another culture?" or "What is the most far-fetched explanation for this problem you can think of?" can be of help in mobilizing clients' imagination.

6

FUTURE VISIONS

A man came every three months to the community mental health center to for an appointment with Ben to renew his prescription. He was a lonely person who lived with his father in a remote house in the countryside. His clothes were shabby, his hair was a mess and he had no teeth. Whenever Ben saw the man he used to kid him about how handsome he would look if he had teeth and fantasize about the girls he could have sitting next to him in his fancy convertible. Ben's wild ideas never failed to amuse the client, but they didn't seem to have any noticeable effect on his physical appearance. About a year after Ben had left the center, he received a postcard from the man which simply said, "Thank you very much—I now have teeth!"

Since the future is often connected to the past, people with a stressful past are prone to have a hopeless view of their future. In its turn a negative vision of the future exacerbates current problems by casting a pessimistic shadow over both past and present.

Fortunately, the converse is also true; a positive view of the future invites hope, and hope in its turn helps to cope with current hardships, to recognize signs indicating the possibility of change, to view the past as an ordeal rather than a misery, and to provide the inspiration for generating solutions.

The following example, provided by Tapani, illustrates how fantasizing about the future helps not only to set goals but also to increase clients' awareness of the solutions they already have.

When the Problem Is Over

I received a crisis phone call from Riina. She said that her husband was on a drinking binge and that they needed urgent help. I learned that alcohol had been a problem to the husband for years. Every few months he would go straight from work to a bar and start drinking with strangers. On these occasions he would stay away from home for days, sometimes for weeks. During his drinking binges he usually kept in touch with his wife by phone.

I asked Riina if her husband was aware that she was calling me. She said that he was, but that he was not interested in family therapy. I said that she could come to meet me without her husband if he preferred not to come. I also suggested that just in case her husband changed his mind they should take a little time before the meeting and entertain the fantasy that their life would be in order. When I met with them we would continue with the idea that we were in the future and I would ask them questions such as "How is your life these days?" and "What do you think made the change possible?"

The next week when I went to their house for the appointment both Riina and her husband Heikki were home. Heikki was suffering from withdrawal symptoms, trembling and perspiring heavily. I asked Heikki if he knew what I had asked them to do before I came. He said that he knew and that he found the suggestion interesting since he had been thinking a lot about the future recently. I asked him, "Well then, how are things now that the problem is over?"

"What do you mean, the problem is over?" said Heikki, who had not yet grasped my idea.

I continued, "Do you remember that we met two years ago? If I remember right, you had some problems with alcohol or something like that. I get the impression that things are OK nowadays, am I right?"

"Yes, Heikki doesn't drink any longer," said Riina, who was eager to enter the fantasy. Heikki then joined in.

"She means that I've reduced the amount I drink, that I only drink a glass or two of wine every now and then."

We developed this imaginary future world for quite some time. As the end of the session drew near I addressed the question of how they explained the change. Heikki said that much of it had to do with the fact that Riina had begun to share the responsibility for family economics. He explained that previously Riina had merely thrown all the bills into a drawer, leaving him to take care of her tax declaration at the end of each year. "For two years now," he said, "she's gathered her bills neatly into piles and completed her declaration all by herself, only asking me for occasional advice." Another explanation that emerged was that Heikki had effected a major change in his working career. He had dreamt for years of doing something radical and now he had finally made his dream come true.

We did not agree upon another appointment. I merely asked Riina and Heikki to give me a call or send me a postcard in order to let me know how things were proceeding. As I was leaving Heikki and Riina seemed optimistic, as if some of the things in the fantasy had actually come true.

I learned later that Heikki actually did fulfil his dream and that he had drastically cut down his drinking.

Positive visions of the future enable people to see their current predicaments as phases in a continuing narrative, where hardships are steps on the path to a better tomorrow. From this viewpoint problems can be perceived as valuable learning experiences and the people involved can be seen as helpers rather than obstacles.

In the following example Tapani invites a teenage girl living at a residential youth home to enter a future vision where the various people in her social network are seen as helpers.

The Helpful Math Teacher

I was invited to teach a one-day workshop on family therapy to the staff of a residential treatment home for adolescents. As we started the day I said that in my opinion the best way to learn was to work with actual cases rather than have theoretical lectures.

The staff said that unfortunately most of their teenagers had been sent home for the day; in fact, there were only two youngsters present, a 17-year-old boy, Risto, and a 14-year-old girl, Minna. I asked the staff if they would like to invite either one of them for a demonstration session. They discussed this possibility for a while and ended up talking about Minna, who had been placed in the home because of truancy and running away from home. She had also had violent conflicts with her mother with whom she was totally at odds. The staff had found Minna to be likable, but she had already earned the reputation of being antagonistic.

I explained: "If we are going to talk about Minna, couldn't we ask her to be present? In my experience it is beneficial for youngsters to hear what is said about them. I've also found that it is often useful to ask their friends to come along. Do you think we could invite Risto to join us?"

My suggestion of inviting Risto to accompany Minna was not received with great enthusiasm. The issue of confidentiality was raised and the staff wondered whether it would be ethically justifiable to have Risto take part in such a conversation. I explained that confidentiality would not pose much of a problem since we would be focusing on the future and we would of course ask for Minna's permission.

The staff added that there was another objection to inviting Risto to come along to the session. They explained that he was known for an inclination to incite new residents into wrongdoing and for that reason it was not considered a good idea for these two youngsters to get to know each other too well.

I persisted and said that I would like to talk with Minna myself so I could ask her opinion about inviting Risto to join us.

The staff agreed and showed me to Minna's room. I introduced myself to her and explained that we were about to discuss her in our consultation meeting and told her that I believed it would be useful for her to come and listen to what we would say about her. She said, "All right, I'll come, but only if I don't have to say anything. I hate being the center of attention."

"Yes, I know how you feel and that's why I suggest that we invite Risto along as well. Would that be OK with you?"

"That's fine with me," she said. I then went to talk to Risto. I told him that we were going to have a meeting in order to talk about Minna's future and that we wanted to invite him to join us. He said, not unlike Minna, that he would come if he could just be an observer.

When everyone was present I explained that it is often more useful to talk about the future than the past and suggested that we take a look at how Minna's future would look without problems. "Let's imagine," I said, "that a year has gone by and we all meet somewhere in the town, perhaps in a cafeteria down the road. The sun is shining and to our surprise Minna walks in. She tells us that everything is fine in her life. What would you tell us, Minna?"

"I can't imagine," she said.

"Well, how about you," I said to Minna's designated nurse, "what do you imagine she'd tell us?"

"She'd say she's back at school," said the nurse.

This opening statement launched a collective fantasy

in which Minna was doing well at school and getting along better than ever with her parents and friends. When someone said that she would have good grades in math I noticed a wry look on her face. "Well, how does that sound to you? Good grades in math, eh?"

"Sounds completely impossible to me," she said.

"Let's just imagine that you are indeed doing well even in math. Hearing about that I would be very curious to know what made it possible. How did this come about? What would Minna say?"

"She began to do her homework," said someone from the staff.

"I don't think I'll ever be good at math," said Minna.

"How about Risto, is he good at math?" I asked.

"As a matter of fact he is," said the director of the home.

"In that case, could it be that Risto has been helping Minna with math?" I proposed. Risto's face showed traces of a smile. I turned to Minna and said, "Well, could that be possible?"

"I guess it could," she said, smiling.

"Suppose he turned out to be a really demanding teacher who made you work and gave you homework every day. Would you do what he told you to do?" I asked Minna.

"I just might," she said.

"Well, Risto? Would you help Minna with math?"

"Who knows?" he said.

As well as school we talked also about other aspects of Minna's positive future. She gradually became an active participant in the conversation and said, among other things, that she would once again be on good terms with her mother and that she would have kept the same boyfriend as well as having found many new friends.

Having heard about her boyfriend, I said, "Oh, I didn't know you had a boyfriend. What's his name?"

"None of your business," Minna said with a confident smile.

"You could at least reveal the first letter of his name," I said gently teasing her.

"It starts with the letter M," she said and added, "but don't think I'll tell you more."

I could not resist the temptation to continue but there was no way of making Minna volunteer her boyfriend's name. I then changed the subject and asked her, "What will be the things that tell people that you've got your life together again?"

"I will have a cat and many hobbies," said Minna.

"That sounds good," I said and explained that in my experience it is always a favorable sign when people have specific plans for the future. Before we ended the session I said that I would be very interested to meet her again after a year to find out how things have developed. Also, since I didn't know whether I would be coming again, I invited her to send me a postcard or a letter to catch up on how things were going. Minna agreed to send me a postcard and I gave her my address as we closed the session.

Interestingly, during the coffee break after the session Risto came over to talk to me. He asked whether it was possible to arrange a similar "future planning session" for him as well. I regretted that I did not have enough time for another session that day and suggested that, as he and the staff now knew the procedure, they could do it together without me.

About six months later I received a letter from Minna. This is what she wrote:

"Hello Tapani, how have you been? I have been quite OK. School is going well, my scores were good and in other ways my life has become regular. The name of my boyfriend still begins with an M. Now I can tell you his name. His name is Mika. I have a job through June right here at the residential home. In July I'll be home on holiday with my family. In early August I have a discharge negotiation. I will return to my old school. There have been other changes in our family as well. For example, mother and I can now talk about anything, we have moved to a new flat and I follow the rules. I have a kitten.

Its name is Jonna. Mother will take care of it while I am working here. When I'm at home I often go swimming, take the dog out and play with the cat. I have many friends, three girls and seven boys. Our mother has also found herself a new friend. Hope to see you sometime. I guess that's all for now. Enjoy the rest of your summer vacation. Take care, Minna."

There are many other ways of inviting clients to fantasize about a positive future apart from simply asking them to imagine their future without the problem. One such method developed by Steve de Shazer and his team is known as the "miracle question." Here clients are asked to imagine how their life would be if their problems miraculously disappeared overnight. There are countless ways of asking people to think about a positive future, for instance:

"Imagine that a year has passed and you decide to send us a postcard with good news. What would the good news be?"

"If someone were to bring me good news about you in the future, what would they tell me?"

"Let's say your therapist had a dream one night in which you were happy and doing fine. What kind of a dream would it be?"

"If you imagine your life is like a novel and the next chapter is a happy one, what will happen in it?"

In one of our consultation sessions we talked to a 17-year-old girl who came in for a consultation with her classmate, her teacher, the principal of the boarding school, and the matron of the dormitory. She had a variety of problems with several of her teachers and there were a number of conflicts in the dormitory. She also had difficulties with her family and had not been on speaking terms with her father for more than a year.

During the session we invited the girl to imagine that one day in the future when school is part of her past, she decides to write a letter to tell her former teachers how she is doing. Everyone in the group collaborated in the writing of this imaginary letter, in which she wrote that she was now employed as a nurse in Bogota, Colombia, and that she was enjoying the work. She had learned to speak fluent Spanish, and in contrast to the time when she was at college, she was now on relatively good terms with her father. In the letter she also thanked her teacher, the principal and her former classmates for their tolerance and help in dealing with her problems.

We suggested to her that she might also write that having had problems at school and gaining the experience of being met halfway by others had helped her to find a way of getting along better with her father. She thought about it for a while and then said, "Could be."

In the following example Ben uses the miracle question to invite a depressed woman to find a new way of thinking about her life.

The Lady Who Had Catered for the President

Sirkka, who was a psychiatric nurse, participated in one of our training groups. She brought to the session Emma, a middle-aged unmarried woman who was a patient on her ward at the local psychiatric hospital. She had also invited several members of the staff, a physician, a social worker, the head nurse of the ward, and the patient's designated nurse to join the session.

We learned that Emma had been in various psychiatric hospitals for most of the past six years because of what had been diagnosed as major depression. The current problem, from the staff's point of view, was that she complained all the time and refused to talk about anything but her misfortune and her misery.

I invited Emma to think about her future by asking, "What will your life be like when this misery is over?"

"Oh, it'll never be over," she said.

"Let's imagine that it will. How would your life look then?" I persisted.

"I can't even imagine such a thing," she said bluntly.

"I understand that," I said courteously, "but let's imagine that a miracle takes place one night and that you wake up in the morning and the problems are gone. How would you know that a miracle had occurred?"

Emma thought for a moment and then said softly, "This awful anguish in my chest would be gone."

"You'd wake up in the morning, you'd notice that the anguish is gone, then what would you do next?" I continued.

"I don't know. I guess I'd go to the hairdresser," she said. This statement opened a discussion about her future. We imagined that after her recovery she would soon return home. When she was asked about what she would do when she was back at home, Emma said she might consider taking up the job she used to have. The group was curious to know what she had done before her "illness." It emerged that she used to have her own small catering business and that she had been so well respected that when the former president visited her town she had been asked to take charge of the catering arrangements. The excellence of her former reputation was confirmed by several members of staff.

The group joined the discussion and questioned Emma about her past. She took pride in her answers and the discussion about the subject of "life before the illness" had a remarkable effect on her appearance. She no longer looked like a chronically depressed patient from a psychiatric hospital, but like a dignified and capable woman.

At the end of the session I asked all present whether they thought that talking about future visions and past successes were subjects worth further discussion on the ward. Both Emma and the staff agreed with the recommendation.

When everyone was getting ready to leave, one of the male psychologists in the group politely helped Emma to put on her coat and she was more than pleased.

A year later I was once again teaching a course in the same town. One of the participants was a nurse in the same hospital where Emma had been in treatment. She reported that soon after the session Emma had moved into a house of her own and had not returned to the hospital. In addition, the nurse had heard that Emma had helped in the recovery of another patient. She said she had been wondering about what had happened at the consultation. She had been on duty on the evening of the session and when Emma returned to the ward she had spoken about nothing else but the fact that a psychologist had helped her with her coat.

Most people enjoy fantasizing about the future and will readily agree when it is suggested by the therapist. On occasion, however, people seem either unable or unwilling to generate positive visions of the future.

When this happens the therapist can construct his or her own fantasies about the client's future and share these by letting the client comment on the vision. When there are several people present in the session, such as friends, family members, or other helpers, it is possible to invite them to offer their positive future fantasies concerning the client. Hearing other people's fantasies about their future compels clients to become involved.

The following story, drawn from Tapani's work as the supervisor of a team of social welfare workers, illustrates this point.

The Clean T-shirt

The team asked me for ideas of how to handle their homeless alcoholics, who regularly came to pick up their welfare checks but refused to go to residential treatment centers for alcoholics. I suggested that we arrange a meeting with these people as a group so that they could be encouraged to help one another. The next time I came to the office there was a group of 14 men and one woman. Their clothes were dirty and there was an odor in the room

but they appeared to be a friendly and humorous group of
people. I greeted them and explained that I was there to
consult with the social workers.

The atmosphere was playful and there was a lot of kid-
ding about, something these people seemed to be at home
with. I first addressed Sam, a man in ragged clothes who
had been drinking for years. I asked him to fantasize how
life would look to him after a year if things developed for
the better.

"I don't have the faintest idea," said Sam, who had apparently given up dreaming about a positive future a long
time ago. Fortunately, many of the other people present
knew him well and came to his rescue. One man said the
only thing in the world that would make Sam stop drinking was for him to become a born-again Christian. Another man added that a good woman was needed to change
him; this provoked merriment in the group. Someone else
added that before any woman could ever become interested in Sam he would have to be clean and start wearing
cleaner clothes. All these imaginative suggestions compelled Sam to join in the fantasizing about his future, so
much so that all of a sudden he put his hand into his bag
and pulled out a clean t-shirt. He showed it to the group
and said that he always carried it with him just in case he
might need it one day.

When clients hold a pessimistic view of the future, it may
prove useful to start off by first generating a negative future
vision. The completion of the gloomy future fantasy paves the
way for the possibility of a positive vision. Even in cases where
the only thing a client can see in the future is suicide, the
therapist can pursue a positive future vision by building upon
the client's suicide fantasy. After having established a good
rapport with the client, the therapist might say, for example,
"Suppose that after you die you find yourself at the heavenly
gates. You are greeted in a respectful manner by an angel who
informs you that your case has been reconsidered and that you
have been granted a second chance. When you return to earth

you find that your problems are gone and that your life is quite satisfactory. How would life be for you then?"

In some cases it is worth creating more that one future vision. For example, with couples who are considering divorce it may prove useful to generate at least two future visions, one involving separation and the other involving staying together. These visions are allowed to develop until they become positive. Openings should also be left for "further options," even if only represented by a symbolic question mark on the flip board onto which the alternative visions are recorded.

The idea of leaving openings for additional alternatives is based on the fact that, when two or more people are in conflict with one another, neither of them is likely to accept the other's point of view, nor are they likely to agree on a compromise that lies somewhere in the middle. Often a resolution of the conflict involves a "third alternative" that both parties see as being quite different from the original conflicting propositions. The generation of multiple visions favors the emergence of such third alternatives.

The following example illustrates how multiple visions can help when working with clients who have conflicting expectations of the future.

Amor's Choice

We received a phone call from a youth crisis shelter, the staff of which had trained with us some time previously. We were asked to come to conduct a session on the case of a 14-year-old girl, Ami, who had sought refuge at the shelter because of a conflict between her and her mother. There had already been one meeting at the shelter with both mother and daughter present. According to the staff, this meeting had turned into a disaster; mother and Ami had engaged in a furious argument, during which mother had threatened Ami with both violence and suicide. In spite of this, a second meeting had been scheduled and to this meeting the staff had also invited father (who had been separated from the family for some years), Ami's 11-year-old sister, and the social worker from the child protection department who was legally in charge of the case. In the staff's opinion mother had been harsh and uncompromising at the previous session. They now expected us to try and help her negotiate more constructively with Ami.

All the parties invited turned up. The atmosphere in room was extremely tense and communication between Ami and her parents was at times openly hostile. We learned that Ami had recently become involved with a 24-year-old man, Amor, who was married and had a six-year-old son. Neither of the parents approved of this relationship. Father knew Amor and claimed that the man was untrustworthy and that he had criminal tendencies. Father gave his complete support to mother's demand that Ami unconditionally put an end to her relationship with Amor. Ami cried and shouted, "You don't understand anything. I care about Amor and he cares about me. I will never leave him. Everything you say about him is a lie!"

In this antagonistic atmosphere we made several unsuccessful attempts at mediation between Ami and her parents. We suggested, for example, that Ami return home and only meet with Amor in the future under her mother's supervision, but neither party accepted this suggestion. We even suggested that Ami should stop seeing Amor altogether, but would maintain the friendship through telephone contact. This proposal was also rejected. Ami protested that she would not give up Amor and the parents repeated that there were no conditions under which they would allow her to have any contact with this married man.

Since it appeared that there was no way of reaching any kind of compromise, we decided to change the subject and talk about alternatives for the future. We suggested the metaphor that Ami was now at a crossroads in her life and that there were at least two different roads to take. This view was accepted by all parties, with the result that the atmosphere in the room became more tolerable. We explained that it seemed to us that one of the two possible options was the way of the parents. According to this alternative Ami would return home to her mother, stop being away from home overnight, stick to her curfew, and renounce Amor. The other option was Ami's way, which meant that she would continue her relationship with Amor. In this case, as the parents had already explained, they would report Ami to the police. The parents would then demand that Amor together with his wife take custody of Ami (in their anger the parents had said this even though they knew quite well that it was an impossible option). If Amor refused, Ami would be taken into custody by the child protection department and placed in a residential youth home. We then invited the family to think further about what would happen after Ami had been placed in the youth home.

"In this vision Ami would be placed by the child welfare worker in a youth home," we said and asked the parents, "Suppose the staff called you and asked you to attend a family session? Would you go?"

"No we wouldn't," said the parents.

"What about if, after some years when things have cooled down, they invited you to join her sixteenth birthday party. Would you then consider going?"

"We might consider that," said the parents matter-of-factly.

We concluded that there were at least two, perhaps more, ways to proceed. One option was for Ami to return home and forget about Amor. The other option was for Ami to keep up the contact with Amor, be placed in a youth home, and over the years gradually become friendly with her parents once again.

At this point we proposed ending the session. The family members thanked us upon leaving even though little if nothing had been achieved at this point. After the session we spoke with the staff and suggested that they invite

Amor to the shelter in order to make him take a stand concerning the available options.

The staff followed our suggestion. The same evening they managed to contact Amor and invited him to the shelter. Amor accepted the invitation and came at once. The staff reviewed with Ami and him the alternatives outlined in our consultation session. He declared that there was no way for him to take responsibility for bringing up Ami. He also said that following a recent serious discussion with his wife he was planning to return to his family.

The following day Ami got herself an immediate placement at a youth home. She stayed there two weeks and then returned home to her mother and agreed to follow the rules.

Discussing positive visions of the future can be useful in many ways. They give people something to aspire to, they foster optimism, and they help in the setting of goals. With a positive vision of the future we are able to view our past as a resource, to recognize and value progress that is already underway, to see other people as allies rather than adversaries, and to think of our problems as ordeals that can contribute to the struggle to reach our goals.

The future is perhaps one of the most gratifying subjects for therapeutic conversations. It is a country which no one can own and which is therefore open to all possible ideas and imaginings. People have different ideas about what lies in the future, and they may disagree about what it should bring, but since people know deep down that no one can ultimately know what the future will bring, it is a wonderful place for constructive conversations.

7

BUILDING ON PROGRESS

Positive Coaching

At the age of nine Tapani's son began to play soccer. The team he played on had no coach and Tapani was asked to sign up for the job. Although he had no previous experience in soccer he did not want to refuse for the sake of his son.

Standing at the side of the soccer field for the very first time, he didn't know what to do. He observed the more experienced coaches, who shouted to the boys things such as, "Watch the sides!" "Stay on-side!" and "Pass, pass, pass, don't sit on the ball!"

Before long he was shouting just like the other coaches about the things that the boys were supposed to do and criticizing them for things they weren't supposed to do. It didn't take long for him to realize that all his shouting was not having much effect. No matter how much or how loud he yelled, the boys would not pass the ball to one another as a soccer team should. Eventually, trying to avoid feeling like a fool, he decided to change track. Instead of criticizing the boys he decided to try and encourage them.

In the next game the boys played much as usual. Tapani kept quiet throughout the first half but at half-time he said, "Boys, I'm proud of you. I noticed that many times during the game you were going to pass the ball!"

The boys eagerly agreed. One of them said that he had

been about to pass several times but that each time someone else had been in the way.

During the second half the boys passed the ball to one
another significantly more often; when the game was over
Tapani acknowledged this development. He also said to
them, "You're fortunate to play on a losing team. Losing is
an excellent way to learn soccer and many very good players have started off playing on a losing team. Also, losing
teams tend to have a good team spirit, right?"

The boys grew fond of playing in the team while Tapani
grew fond of soccer and the team. Tapani is now a soccer
enthusiast and most weekends he is off playing with his
now winning team.

If asked, people who come to talk with professionals about
their problems will more often than not report that some
progress has already taken place. This phenomenon is known
as "pretreatment change" (Weiner-Davis, de Shazer, &
Gingerich, 1987) and is at the heart of solution-focused therapy
as described by Steve de Shazer and his group in Milwaukee (de
Shazer, 1991). The reader will find the theme of progress in one
form or another in most of the case examples in this book.

Talking about improvement—whether minimal or substantial, temporary or enduring—is an agreeable subject which has
an encouraging effect on people.

Ben once worked on an adolescent ward in a psychiatric
hospital where family therapy (Milan style) was used as
part of treatment. An integral part of this form of therapy
is the giving of compliments to families. One day a nurse
who frequently participated in the family therapy sessions suggested that the giving of compliments was
something that could perhaps be used more widely with
the adolescents on the ward. The idea soon crystallized
into a practical suggestion; at the end of each week, a
group session would be held during which the staff would
give compliments to the patients for their accomplishments over the preceding week.

In contrast to conventional group therapy, which tends to focus on problems, this session soon became quite popular and became known as the "Friday morning group." Two staff members met before each session and prepared positive feedback for each of the adolescents. There was always something good to say about everyone even at times when it seemed that an adolescent had experienced nothing but problems in the previous week. For example, two nurses preparing for the session were considering what to say to a teenage girl who had been extremely anxious during the week. She had been sitting on the floor whining for hours on end and had at times even bounced her head against the wall. The nurses concluded that, despite her behavior, she had in fact made progress in coping with her anxiety. On many previous occasions when she had been overwhelmed by such extreme anxiety she had slashed her wrists and attempted to take her life. When the nurses told her of this indication of progress at the Friday morning session, she smiled and appeared pleased.

The Friday morning group was started several years ago and the ward has since witnessed many changes, but over the years this progress-focused activity has occupied a central role in the overall treatment.

A school teacher who had attended a workshop on the use of solution-oriented methods with children provided another example of the beneficial effects of focusing on progress. After the workshop she went to talk with her headmaster about the need to focus on progress rather than problems. As a result of this conversation the headmaster decided to organize a special teachers' meeting at which each teacher would be invited to relate a story describing one of her/his successes with the pupils.

At the subsequent meeting each teacher had a story to tell. Charming stories were told and everyone listened with keen interest. At the end of the meeting many of the teachers remarked that they would like to do this more often.

When there is evidence of progress, even if it is meager, talking about it allows the conversation to move naturally towards such constructive subjects as what made the improvement possible and who did what to bring it about.

In the following example, Ben, simply by being curious about progress, apparently succeeds in encouraging a change that is already taking place.

Therapeutic Research

A mother called me and wanted to bring her 12-year-old son, Kim, to me for a consultation. It emerged that Kim had a variety of behavioral problems both at home and at school. His disruptive behavior had led to his transfer from the ordinary class to a special class.

Before mother had completed her detailed report of Kim's problems, I asked her if there were any recent signs of progress. She answered in the affirmative and offered some evidence of improvement.

I said, "Since there seems to be some movement in the right direction, may I suggest that you do some research before we agree on an appointment. Would you agree?"

"What am I supposed to do?" she asked.

"You should go to each member of your family and the teacher, tell them about Kim's improvement, and then ask them what is their explanation for it. Call me back in a week or so, and let me know what they have said. That's all you need to do for now. We can discuss the appointment when you call me again."

The mother accepted the task and called me back a week later. She reported that improvement had continued and that she had obtained some answers. In her husband's opinion the improvement had taken place because he had stopped putting pressure on Kim. The elder brother had said that he had invited Kim to join him and his friends. The teacher had explained that he had recently started a class project that had produced positive reaction from all of his pupils.

"How about yourself, do you agree with any of these explanations?" I asked.

"No, I don't," she said. "I think the real reason is that my husband has recently been giving in to Kim's every whim. Things are all right when Kim gets his way, but what the boy really needs is limits."

Without taking too much notice of the fact that she apparently held her husband responsible for the problem, I asked, "How about Kim himself? Did he have an explanation for his progress?"

"Oh, I didn't ask him," said mother regretfully.

"In that case what you could do is to continue a little bit with this research. May I suggest that you now go to Kim and tell him that you've been impressed by his recent progress and that everyone else has noticed it. You could then tell him about your research and reveal the answers to him, including your own explanation. You could ask him whether he agrees with any of those explanations or if he has an explanation of his own. The purpose here is to get Kim, your family members, and Kim's teacher to think and talk about the progress that has been achieved."

Mother accepted the task and agreed to call me again. After several weeks she called me and said that Kim had continued to improve to the point where she felt that there was no longer any need to make an appointment.

Focusing on progress achieved leads very naturally to the question of how it should be explained; this in turn is a rich source of information about what has been helpful so far. Clients' own ideas about what has helped them can be used as a starting point from which to develop future plans.

This principle is illustrated in the following story, which dates back to one of our first training programs.

Climatotherapy

A social worker brought in a couple for consultation. The wife, who was suffering from depression, had been discharged from a psychiatric hospital only a week previously. At the beginning of the interview the therapist discovered that the wife had made some progress. When asked for her own explanation of her recovery she answered that the weather had been better lately. Her husband nodded in agreement. It was found that the couple was convinced beyond doubt that the problems in the wife's moods were caused by problems in the climate. The therapist was reluctant to countenance this explanation, so we asked her to join us for a brief discussion in the observation room. During this conversation we invited her to accept the unusual climatological explanation at face value. After all, we argued, it was just as valid as any psychological hypothesis that we professionals might have come up with. The therapist agreed and spent the rest of the session talking with the couple about the weather and its influences. At the end of the session, as we had agreed, the therapist suggested that the couple would take detailed daily notes of the weather conditions: temperature, atmospheric pressure and humidity. On the same chart they were to report details of their prevailing moods. The justification for this task was to learn more about the way the climate affected their moods.

The follow-up showed that the couple had carefully completed the task. After reading the charts they had concluded that the climate didn't have as much influence on their mood as they had believed. Despite this observation progress had continued and the couple seemed pleased with the therapy they were receiving.

The following example, provided by Ben, illustrates how the theme of progress easily leads to discussions about how other people, in this case parents, can support the ongoing change.

The Shy Typist

Sirkka was a gentle, shy woman in her early twenties. She came in for consultation accompanied by her elder sister who had made the appointment. After learning that she lived with her boyfriend near her parents' house and worked as a typist, I asked Sirkka what brought her to see me. She explained that she was afraid of people. This problem had begun at the age of 17 and had grown to such intensity that she had been forced to leave high school – in spite of the fact that she had been a successful pupil determined to head for university. After Sirkka left school, her mother had helped her to get work as a typist.

Going to work was extremely trying for Sirkka. As much as possible she avoided contact with others and lived with the constant fear that she might be asked to join them for coffee, lunch or evenings out. Recently Sirkka had spent much of her time at home crying and the thought of suicide had even entered her mind. Some time ago Sirkka's sister had read an article about panic disorder and she had persuaded Sirkka to consult a psychiatrist in the hope that medication could be of help.

At the end of the first session I suggested that Sirkka should bring her parents with her to the following session. She raised no objection and even her sister, who expressed concern about Sirkka's close relationship with her parents, thought that it was a good idea. Sirkka suspected that her parents would not agree to come, but I tried to persuade her by saying with a smile, "If they are hesitant just tell them that I am an old-fashioned psychiatrist who still believes that parents are the best people to help their children."

Sirkka arrived at the next session with her parents. As soon as everyone was comfortable I asked whether there had been any recent progress. Sirkka proudly explained that an old friend who lived nearby had invited her to play in a basketball game. Sirkka had been an ardent basketball player at school and had agreed to go. She had enjoyed the game even though she had avoided talking with the other players. On her way home she and her friend had discussed the possibility of playing basketball on a more regular basis.

Hearing of Sirkka's progress prompted mother to recall her own youth when she had suffered from a similar problem. The mother explained that she had gradually conquered her timidity by determinedly entering frightening situations.

"That's right," I agreed with mother. "I also think that the way to overcome these kinds of problems is to start doing the things one has been afraid of, just as Sirkka has begun to do. Our role is to offer support and encouragement."

"How could we encourage her?" asked father.

"It's easier said than done, isn't it?" I agreed, "and it's particularly difficult to encourage your own adult children. Whatever you say may be interpreted as intrusiveness rather than support."

This point was well received by everyone. I then proceeded to relate the story about how Tapani found a way to encourage the boys in his soccer team to pass the ball to one another. They all enjoyed the story. Father said that he now better understood what Sirkka's problem was all about.

I said to the parents, "If you wish to encourage Sirkka, why not consider doing something along the same lines as Tapani. For example, every day when Sirkka comes home from work ask her if at any point during the day she considered doing something courageous. Putting the question in this way should allow her to answer in the affirmative." Turning to Sirkka, I said, "Would you agree that every day at work you have the intention of doing something in the right direction—such as talking with someone, joining the others for coffee, or planning to return to your studies—even if you don't always do anything tangible?"

"Yes, I always think of doing something like that," agreed Sirkka.

"All right, let me then suggest that every day when Sirkka comes home from work you ask her, 'Did you intend to do something today?' Sirkka should then respond by saying 'Yes.' After this you should encourage her in a way that she feels is encouraging."

"But what should we say after she says 'yes'?" asked mother.

"You might say something such as, 'That's good,' or 'That's wonderful.' How about it, Sirkka? Would you take that as encouragement?"

"No, I wouldn't," said Sirkka.

"Well, what would you like them to do? Should they just keep quiet, give you a kiss, or what?"

"Perhaps they shouldn't say anything."

"What about them giving you a hug? Would that encourage you?"

Sirkka thought for a while and then said, "It might be better, but my parents haven't hugged me in years."

I asked mother, "Well, would you mind giving Sirkka a hug for her 'yes' answer?"

Mother smiled affectionately and said, "Why not, I guess it wouldn't hurt her."

"Only if you squeeze too hard," I said with a smile and then turned to father, "What about you, what do you think about this idea of giving Sirkka a hug?"

"Well . . . ," he said with a troubled look on his face. It is not all too common for fathers to hug their adult daughters here in Finland.

"What about tapping her like this," I said and tapped Sirkka on her shoulder in the way a teacher would do to encourage a child.

"That's OK with me," he said.

I then suggested that the parents rehearse this task there and then. Mother asked Sirkka if she had intended to do something courageous. Sirkka said "yes," whereupon mother gave her a big hug. They both laughed.

Then it was father's turn. With a little help from me he managed to ask the same question and received a "Yes" for his answer. He went up to Sirkka and was just about to tap her on the shoulder when he changed his mind and gave her a quick but affectionate hug. We all laughed.

I met Sirkka twice more and talked with her on the phone a couple of times in the next year. She made steady progress and eventually felt capable of continuing on her own without further therapy.

The subject of progress functions as a springboard for the discovery of new solutions. The following example, told by Ben, illustrates how progress can present a pathway leading away from problems and towards concrete plans for the future.

Project Plan

Hessu made an appointment because his best friend, who was worried about his condition, had advised him to see a psychiatrist. His problems had started soon after he and his wife had divorced a few years previously. His wife was still bitter and not only refused to have any contact with him but also refused to let him see his daughter. Hessu drank to excess and was frustrated in his job as a manager of large-scale construction projects. On top of everything else he had recently been spurned by his steady girlfriend.

"You don't appear to be all that miserable. Has there been some recent progress?" I asked.

"As a matter of fact, I have been able to somewhat cut down on my drinking," said Hessu. "After talking with my best friend I realized that I cannot go on this way."

We talked about Hessu's progress and about his work in project planning. I learned that Hessu was skillful at his job, which involved huge projects. He had received offers of several excellent positions, but he had turned them all down because he was afraid that his poor emotional state would incapacitate him.

"It seems to me that the project of improving the quality of your life is already well underway," I said. "The only thing that is lacking is a clear project plan."

As Hessu agreed with this view I went on, "What you might do is draw up a project plan for your future. This plan should cover each of the areas of your life that you need to improve. It should include information about your goals, about what you have already achieved and what still needs to be done. Do it just in the way that you do your project plans at work."

At the next session Hessu presented an impressive three page typewritten project plan entitled THE REST OF MY LIFE. It was made up of five separate sections; "Drinking," "Resources," "My relationship with my daughter," "Women and future family," and "Friends." The following excerpt is drawn from the section on resources:

2. RESOURCES

2.1. Starting point

I feel my batteries are flat. My existence feels like a black hole; it's minute, it sucks all radiation from the outside into its dark center and allows no radiation to escape. I haven't been able to accept new challenges in my work, I have difficulties in continuing my studies, going to the movies feels like a compulsive escape from reality, I am unable to concentrate on reading, I have given up my more worthwhile hobbies such as volleyball and aikido.

2.2. Desires

To become more active. A higher level of activity would guarantee more extensive utilization of my potential resources.

2.3. Potential

My potential resources are good. I am well educated (at least formally), I have challenging hobbies and my physical health is good.

2.4. Goals

I will attempt to obtain increased satisfaction from my work or I will try to find a job that can give me more satisfaction. I will attempt to return to several pastimes, such as reading, going to the movies, and attending concerts. Hiking in Lapland and similar activities have become important to me. They keep me fit, both physically and psychologically. I will also attempt to improve my health by biking and going to the gym. It would be fun to begin volleyball and aikido again.

The session was spent in detailed scrutiny of Hessu's project plan and our discussion led to several minor additions. I met Hessu twice more that fall. I then heard nothing more from him until the following summer, when he called to invite me to join him and a small group of other people, including some of our mutual friends, on a weekend hiking trip. I was sorry I had to turn down the invitation because of other obligations.

The following example illustrates how sticking to the theme of progress highlights the client's own resources and the positive aspects of close relationships.

User's Guide to Child Welfare

On a trip to the United States we were offered an opportunity to give a lecture to the staff of the outpatient clinic of a psychiatric hospital. After the lecture Carlos, a young resident in psychiatry, invited us to join him for a therapy session with a client.

Carlos introduced us to the patient, Maggie, and gave us some background. We learned that Carlos had met Maggie some half a dozen times. She had been referred to him by a child welfare social worker who felt that Maggie needed psychiatric help to cope with her problems.

Maggie was a single parent who in the past year had experienced great difficulties in taking care of her two small children. The children had been taken into custody and placed in another family for a period of time. Recently, partly as a result of Maggie's good collaboration with her social worker, the children had returned home.

Maggie told us that the social worker, who had been of

much support to her, was almost like a friend. For example, some time previously she had felt so exhausted that she came to the conclusion that she was truly unable to care for her children. She had decided to place them in custody until she felt capable of taking care of them again. Her social worker had accepted her request and the children had been placed in foster care for a period of two weeks. During this time Maggie had regained her strength after which she was given the children back.

"That's quite an accomplishment," said Ben. "You have overcome your depression and regained your children. You've even made friends with your social worker. Amazing! How do you explain all this? Would you say talking to Dr. Carlos has been of help?"

"Oh, yes," said Maggie. "He's been wonderful. I don't know how I would ever have made it without him."

"What's so wonderful about him?" Tapani said with a smile. "He looks pretty ordinary to me."

Tapani's question provoked Maggie into praising Carlos. She spoke so well of him that he appeared embarrassed.

"I'm sorry about this, Carlos," Tapani continued jokingly, "but if this is difficult to listen to then you can hide in the closet and stay there until we have finished." Carlos smiled and decided to stay.

After Carlos had, in his turn, complimented Maggie for her honesty and her collaborative spirit, we brought up the fact that Maggie had been able to establish a good working relationship with her child welfare social worker.

"It's splendid that you have become friends with your social worker," complimented Ben. "In our experience, on many occasions people end up in an adversarial relationship with child welfare officials. We are curious to know your secret."

"Always tell them the truth," explained Maggie. "I've found that there is no point in cheating. I trust her and she trusts me."

"That's a fine principle," continued Ben, "but I bet there

is much more you could say about how to collaborate with child welfare officials for your own benefit."

It emerged that Maggie had a philosophy about dealing with representatives of the child welfare system. She explained, among other things, that it was of utmost importance to regard social workers as allies rather than enemies. Towards the end of the session Tapani said, "There are so many people throughout the world who could benefit from these principles of yours. Wouldn't it be a good idea for the two of you to write a users' guide for people who have to deal with child welfare social workers? Maggie has firsthand experience and know-how; she could be the consultant while Carlos does the writing. With teamwork like yours the book might well turn out to be a best-seller."

Carlos found the idea appealing. He remarked that there was indeed a real demand for such a book. We concluded the session with a recommendation that Carlos write a letter to Maggie's child welfare social worker to let her know of Maggie's progress and thank her for contributing to it.

Focusing on progress and improvement is more than just a therapeutic technique of identifying factors contributing to a solution. It is a way of encouraging clients' optimism and helping them to adopt a more forward-looking approach to their problems — even life in general. In the following story related by Ben, a client who was utterly focused on her problems was encouraged to adopt a more progress-oriented outlook towards her life.

The Jesus Picture

I received a long distance phone call from a father who wanted to make an appointment for his family. He explained that for many years the family had experienced problems with their daughter, Lilli, who had recently made a very serious attempt at suicide.

Lilli was in her early twenties but looked much younger than her age. She was talkative and appeared to be in a good mood but her parents appeared distressed and sad. I learned that as a teenager Lilli had become preoccupied with her appearance. She had come to believe that there was something wrong with the shape of her nose. What had at first been a teenager's quite normal concern about her looks had gradually become the center of her life. Lilli had insisted on having a nose operation and mother had finally complied after having obtained approval from a psychiatrist. Lilli had not been satisfied with the result of the operation and her obsession with her nose became more intense. She also became resentful to her mother and the psychiatrist for allowing her to proceed with the operation. She attempted suicide twice, was hospitalized for a period, and began to attend regular psychotherapy. When she was at home she spent most of her time discussing her nose and talking about killing herself.

In spite of these problems Lilli did remarkably well in school and graduated with excellent grades. She entered university but made almost no progress at all. In her second year Lilli made yet another suicide attempt, her most serious so far. Against all the odds she survived.

After obtaining this information the parents asked me how they should respond to Lilli's threats of suicide, since mother currently spent 24 hours a day at Lilli's side to keep an eye on her. When they were together mother and Lilli argued with each other most of the time and father was worried about how much longer mother could take it. Suggestions that arose for consideration ranged from not paying any attention at all to Lilli when she spoke about suicide, changing the subject, and responding in some unexpected way. We even spoke about quite absurd alternatives, such as startling her by tickling as soon as she brought up the subject of suicide. This last suggestion was actually rehearsed by the family at the session, but even though Lilli seemed to enjoy the tickling, mother doubted that this strategy could succeed in real life.

Some weeks later I received a phone call from father. He reported that the family had been pleased with the session but that there had been no significant improvement in Lilli's behavior. She still talked about killing herself every day and the parents had not been able to find any successful way of responding to her. I invited father to tell Lilli that she could call me or write to me if she wanted to.

Lilli then called me from time to time. She usually started off with a torrent of words about the past, complaining about her nose, her brother, or her parents. I made attempts to change the subject, brought out the good in her parents and tried my best to get her to talk about her future plans and about any recent progress. After a year Lilli wrote to me. She sent me her picture and wrote that her therapist had said that continuing to have contact with me distracted her therapy.

On the wall of my office there was a charming picture of a laughing Jesus, which I had cut out of *Playboy* magazine. It was an illustration that appeared some years earlier in an article by Harvey Cox which portrayed Jesus as a humorous and fun-loving person. I stuck the picture on piece of cardboard and sent it to Lilli with the following note.

"Dear Lilli. Thank you for your letter and the nice picture of yourself. After receiving your letter I thought of an idea of how to help you. I am enclosing a picture. You are to hang it on the wall of your room. It is a healing picture. Look at it a few times daily. When you have recovered send the picture back to me. Along with the picture send me a letter in which you explain how the picture helped you to recover. I will then send the picture to another patient, and with your approval, I will enclose a copy of your letter."

In the letter I also asked her to thank her parents for their patience and her therapist for all the help she had received from her. I also encouraged Lilli to start dreaming about the future, about studying, a profession, boy-friends, etc.

The next week I received a reply from Lilli. It was a photo depicting two burning candles with the following text written on the back, "These could be funeral candles, but if your picture of Jesus Christ brings help I promise to write a letter for you to show to other patients."

I didn't respond to her note but I received another letter from her after about a year. She reported that she was now engaged to a kind man who had been very helpful to her. "He is the best psychiatrist for me," she wrote, "he often tickles me and says, 'If you kill yourself . . . very well, I'll kill myself too!' Can you think of anything nicer to say?!"

She concluded her letter with the following words, "I have learned to enjoy the small moments of life. I cannot, however, give you your picture back just yet, because I love it."

About a year later I spoke with Lilli's father on the phone. He informed me that there had been much progress despite the fact that Lilli still occasionally talked about suicide when in the company of her mother. Some time previously Lilli had married her fiance and she was presently studying at a vocational school in another town.

This chapter has discussed progress and emphasized that it is often possible to find some evidence of improvement and then use that information as a foundation for a constructive therapeutic conversation.

Helpers also face situations where there appears to be steady deterioration or recent setbacks instead of progress. In such situations it is worthwhile to invite clients to make up a fantasy of a positive future before asking about any signs about progress. With a clear positive future visions in mind clients are more likely to be able to see indications of progress in the now. Another possibility is to identify positive aspects of the apparently adverse circumstances. For example, a situation that seems to be getting worse could be approached as providing an opportunity to increase motivation for change or simply as a phase in the recovery process.

The following example demonstrates the idea of a positive approach to setbacks. It is drawn from an experimental project that could well have been called "solution correspondence." In this project, headed by psychologist Tuija Matikka, a team made up of our former trainees corresponded with clients through an electronic mailbox service. In this way clients owning computers who belonged to a specific nationwide bulletin board service could write about their problems and receive advice from the team. The approach used in this case was inspired by Michael White (1984).

Sneaky Poo Strikes Back

The electronic mailbox team received a letter written by a mother who was quite desperate about her four-year-old son, Sami, who had a host of problems, including disobedience, temper tantrums, and soiling. The team responded to her long letter with the following message.

"Thank you very much for your letter. Even though you say that you didn't find it easy to put down these kinds of problems in writing, we feel that you did a good job. Your report was clear and to the point. We believe that this is a good omen.

"You described how Sami has had to endure a number of difficulties, among them surgical operations, frequent shifts in places of care, the birth of another baby, etc. Experts argue whether such ordeals make children stronger or weaker. We believe that such trials are more likely to make children stronger. We get the impression that despite the fact that Sami has problems he is underneath it all a healthy young man. Your letter basically brought up two problems.

"First, there is the problem that Sami is exceptionally stubborn. From what you wrote about the importance of setting limits we get the feeling that you and your husband already know the answer to this problem. Being firm and consistent works wonders in the long run. It seems that Sami has a strong character so it will not hurt him even if he is sent to his room and told to stay there until he can control his behavior.

"Second, we were sorry to hear that Sneaky Poo has crept into your family. He is a sly little devil for which there seems to be no quick and certain cure. Getting rid of him calls for good ideas and close collaboration between your family and the kindergarten staff. Our recommendation is that you gather your family together and inform everyone that the soiling problem is not the fault of Sami, father, mother, baby sister or the staff at the kindergarten because Sneaky Poo alone carries the sole responsibility. You then explain that the purpose of the meeting is to think of ways of sending Sneaky Poo packing.

"We know from experience that getting rid of Sneaky Poo is anything but easy. We will send you by post a copy of "Sneaky Poo comes to stay," a pertinent bedtime story written by an Austrian family therapist (Wernitznig, 1987/88), and hope it will be of help. We wish you luck and look forward to hearing how you get on."

After two weeks mother replied. She thanked the team for the idea of Sneaky Poo and said that she had begun to use it with Sami. She had also explained the idea to the kindergarten staff and they had liked it as well. Initially, Sami had reacted positively to the story about Sneaky Poo using the toilet on several occasions. Sadly, after just a week there was a setback and the problem was now worse than ever.

As evidence of the deterioration mother wrote that when grandmother had taken care of the children the previous Saturday, Sami had refused to go to the toilet, with the result that he had soiled his pants. Mother concluded her message with the following words, "I don't know. Let's see what effect the bedtime story, which I received only

yesterday will have on him. I hope he will be able to concentrate upon it. Too bad that there aren't any pictures.
Well, I guess I will have to draw some myself."

The team responded as follows.

"Your letter was discussed by our training group. They
regretted having forgotten to let you know that Sneaky
Poo typically becomes infuriated when he is discovered.
That is why he now tries everything to strike back with all
his might. However, with all this hassle Sneaky Poo has
truly been exposed. We can now be sure he is to blame for
the problem. When Sneaky Poo fights back it is of the
utmost importance that everyone is united in the struggle
against him. Don't let Sneaky Poo discourage you. In
time, you will be able to send him packing."

After a few weeks we got the following letter from
mother.

"Hello again. At last we have made some progress with
Sami's soiling. I myself decided that I would stop com-
menting upon it, that I would no longer waste so much
energy on it. Whenever I washed Sami's bottom I merely
mentioned in passing that apparently Sneaky Poo had
paid us a visit.

"Last week, Sami unexpectedly announced that from
now on he was going to use the toilet at the kindergarten—and that's precisely what he did. When it appeared
that the problem was over he said, 'It was a long time
before I learned about this.' The change was a wonderful
Christmas present for the kindergarten staff. Christmas
at home went fine and from the beginning of this week
Sami has used the toilet every evening so he has not had
any need to use the toilet at the kindergarten. Soon this
problem will also belong to the past. Thanks."

Progress as well as deterioration are both, to a greater degree than we are accustomed to think, socially constructed phe-
nomena, or even illusions if you like. For progress to take place

there first has to be someone to see it and to speak about it to others.

Tapani was once discussing with his good friend Reni the subject of change. During the conversation Reni said, "Change does not exist until someone sees it."

"What do you mean?" asked Tapani.

"Let me tell you a story," said Reni. "Many years ago I went to several encounter groups. My intention was to observe the process as a psychologist but I soon found that I could not avoid becoming personally involved. In one of the first marathons that I attended the leader asked, at the outset, for participants to share their first impressions about one another. One by one we focused on each group member and gave our impressions. Then it was my turn to hear others' impressions about me. To my absolute bewilderment all of the female participants of the group said one thing in common. They all said I was handsome. This description did not fit with what I had learned to think of myself. Quite spontaneously I asked to leave the session for a minute. I then went and called my mother. I told her what I had just heard about how I look and then asked, 'How is it possible, Mother, that as long as I can remember you have always said that I have no looks at all?' My mother replied, 'I never wanted you to become as stuck up as your father.' I remember that day as the day when I became handsome."

8

SHARING CREDIT

When we were working with a group of special teachers they brought up a question that had been puzzling them for a long time. They said that when disruptive children are removed from their regular classrooms to work part-time under a special teacher in an observation class, most of these children quickly begin to study industriously and behave well. Problems arise when the special teacher reports back favorably about the child's progress: The regular class teacher is usually far from delighted. In fact, according to the special teachers, it frequently happens that the regular teachers begin to pass stricter judgment on pupils after they enter special education, with the result that their performance appears to have deteriorated.

We asked the group what they imagined was the regular teachers' reaction to hearing that a special teacher was getting along fine with a particular pupil. It emerged that the teachers apparently felt blamed; the news that the allegedly disruptive pupil was not causing trouble in the special class seemed to indicate that the problem lay with the teacher rather than the pupil. It became clear that the all too common tension between special teachers and regular teachers derived from an inadvertent rivalry between these two groups of professionals. By its very existence the concept of a special teacher questions the competence of regular teachers to deal with problem pupils. The fact that pupils often rapidly improve their behavior in observation classes serves only to increase this tension further.

As a solution to this problem Tapani suggested that special teachers should first acknowledge that regular teachers may have contributed to whatever improvement has taken place. In their contacts with the regular teacher they should then thank them for their contributions. He said, "When you report back to the regular teachers you might say something like, 'So and so has done remarkably well in my class' and then ask, 'What is it that you've been doing to make it possible?' You can escape the snare of blame by offering credit instead."

Clearly, giving credit to regular teachers has many benefits. It not only improves the relationship between regular teachers and special teachers, but is also likely to have a favorable effect on pupils as they realize that their teachers collaborate and respect one another. Sharing credit also helps people to reduce their skepticism. When regular teachers are given deserved credit for the improvement they become more likely to subscribe to it.

Our discussions with the special teachers gradually led to a more extensive appreciation of the fact that information about improvement can be taken as bad news by those who may be left feeling blamed or disqualified. For example, when the staff of a psychiatric hospital inform the parents that their child has improved during treatment, the parents may feel quite put down. It is as if they are being told, "Your child began to improve as soon as you let us handle him, so there must be something wrong with you." An even more common example of the same phenomenon is when you return home after a period of absence and your spouse informs you that the children have not had any of their usual difficulties during the time you were away!

The following story, told by Ben, aptly illustrates the problem of rivalry and how sharing credit can become a way of resolving it.

Good News Is Bad News

I was conducting a follow-up workshop with a group of preschool teachers who had undergone some earlier training in solution-orientation. During a break one of the preschool teachers came to me and said, "Look, we have been using the positive approach successfully with many parents, but we are currently struggling with a mother who doesn't respond at all. No matter how nice or complimentary we are, she constantly criticizes us and refuses to see anything good in her son."

"Usually people say nice things about you when you say nice things about them," I said, thinking aloud. "What compliments have you given her?"

"We try to say something nice about her son every day when she comes to pick him up, but she never seems glad to hear anything," said the teacher. "For example, the boy has the problem of wetting his pants and just a few days ago I had some really good news. I said to his mother that he had been dry every day at the kindergarten for a whole week. Instead of being pleased with his progress she said – and we find this difficult to understand – that it was because her son was afraid of us. We were all thunderstruck."

"I wonder if you are in some kind of rivalry situation about who is a better mother for him, you or her?" I asked.

"You bet," said the teacher. "Quite often when she comes to pick him up in the afternoon he refuses to leave with her and wants to stay with us instead. Those situations are really embarrassing."

"Does he still wet his pants at home?" I asked.

"Yes. As far as I know there is no improvement at home whatsoever."

The discussion confirmed my feeling that what had been intended as compliments to the mother had actually been received by her as criticism. My recommendation was that the staff should give credit to mother for the fact that her son had learned to control his bladder during the day. The teacher admitted that this made sense and said they would try it.

Implicit blame resulting from improvement may become a problem when two or more parties deal with the same client.

For example, we once visited the geriatric department of a psychiatric hospital. We learned that the staff got along well with their patients but that there were some difficulties in dealing with referring agencies and institutions.

For example, it often happened that patients referred to the geriatric ward because they had problems at the local old people's home either showed no symptoms at all or improved rapidly. However, when the hospital was ready to transfer these patients back to the old people's home, the staff there often refused to believe that any substantial change had taken place. They were therefore reluctant to take the patient back. This dilemma was a source of continual tension between the hospital and the old people's home. We told the staff of our observations about the relationship between teachers and special teachers, pointing out that their dilemma appeared similar. They agreed. We recommended that they begin to share credit for patients' improvement with the staff of the old people's home as a means of enhancing collaboration. Our suggestion was well received.

The following story is drawn from a discussion Ben had with the staff of a psychiatric unit of an institution for the mentally retarded. The primary goal of this discussion was not to develop a suggestion for the presented case, but to find out if and how the ideas of solution talk could possibly be put to work with the mentally retarded.

The Thanks-giving Talisman

Joel was a retarded man who had lived in an institution for most of his life. He had been referred to the psychiatric department a year previously for having frequent fits of loud yelling sometimes accompanied by the throwing and smashing of objects.

During his treatment Joel had made substantial progress. His tantrums had become not only less frequent but also less intense.

The current problem was that it seemed impossible to get Joel transferred back to one of the regular units at the

institution. Joel's tantrums had earned him a dubious reputation and none of the units at the institution were willing to countenance him as a resident. It seemed evident
that a precondition for getting Joel transferred was improvement of his reputation. This was easier said than
done because there were workers on all the units who
knew his story; as a result, everyone knew about Joel's
behavior.

The staff agreed that to improve Joel's reputation they
would have to begin with those workers who knew him.
The prospect of a meeting with these workers at the psychiatric ward where Joel's progress would be discussed
and they would be given some credit for it was, however,
out of the question. The slightest mention of a meeting
concerning Joel would inevitably be understood as an attempt to get him transferred to one of the regular units,
with the certain result that no one would actually show
up.

We then looked for other alternatives. Finally we
thought of an approach that appeared promising. We
devised a novel therapy for tantrums which involved giving the patient a charm bracelet. Each of the small objects on the chain of the bracelet was to be donated by a
person who cared about the patient. The treatment was to
be called "talisman therapy."

To begin this therapy the staff of the psychiatric unit
would approach a number of people who knew Joel and
ask them to help in his treatment by donating a tiny
object as a keepsake. All the objects collected were to be
attached to a chain which was then to be given to Joel
together with the instruction that squeezing it in his fist
would assist him in controlling his outbursts.

We even fantasized that in time rumors about this new
form of treatment would spread around the institution
and variety of versions of "talisman therapy" would become popular. The workers who would have contributed
to Joel's charm bracelet would later be given credit not
only for Joel's improvement, but also for having contrib-

uted to the invention of a new form of therapy particularly suited to the mentally retarded.

At the end of the discussion it was agreed that if indeed
this kind of approach worked it might gradually help to
change Joel's reputation and thereby pave the way for his
eventual transfer. The team decided to give it a try.

Sharing credit is not limited to situations where progress
has already taken place; it also has its place in fantasy, as
illustrated by the following case. The client was an overweight
woman originally referred to a psychologist by a primary
health-care nurse because of depression and suicidal thoughts.
After she had met the psychologist about ten times the client's
depression had begun to lift, but some other problems remained and so the psychologist decided to invite the client to a
consultation session. We helped her devise a positive vision of
the future and towards the end of the session encouraged her to
award credit to all those people who she could imagine had
contributed to making her future vision come true. The session
was conducted by Ben.

The Overweight Lady

I began the interview by inviting Raija, the client, to
make up a future fantasy, "Let's imagine that, say a year
from now, all your problems are over. How do things
look?"

Raija said that she would no longer argue with her
husband about sex. She explained that for quite some
time she had refused sex with her husband and this had
led to frequent rows. Her reason for not wanting to make
love was that being overweight made her feel uncomforta-
ble about sex. She was convinced that she would have to
lose at least 20 kg before that problem could be solved.

There was a woman in the group who was also considerably overweight. She tried to convince Raija that it was
possible to enjoy sex despite being overweight, but to no
avail. Raija insisted that becoming slimmer was the only

way for her. Another participant said half-jokingly that she had read somewhere that sex is one of the most effective ways of losing weight. Raija smiled but was not convinced.

I returned to the future, "Let's imagine that a year has actually gone by and we all happen to see you in the marketplace of your home town. You've lost so much weight that we hardly recognize you. Suddenly, your therapist spots you and says, 'Look there, isn't that Raija? Don't you remember, the lady who came with me to a session a year ago?' Gradually we all make the connection. We ask you to have a cup of coffee with us, and when we're sitting in the sun on a bench with a hot cup of coffee, we ask you how you're doing.

"You proudly inform us that things are fine. We are curious and somebody daringly asks you, 'How is sex with your husband?' and you say, 'Oh sex is fine! These days my husband and I always want to make love at exactly the same time like all normal couples.' We go on to ask you, 'How on earth did you manage that?' and you explain that it was a result of the fact that you lost so much weight. We become even more curious and ask how you succeeded. What do you then say?"

As Raija did not have an answer, I invited the group to provide some ideas.

Someone said, "Perhaps Raija would say that through her therapy with Virpi, she learned to control her life and that helped her to control her weight." Another participant suggested that Raija would say that she decided to go jogging every time her husband complained about her unwillingness to have sex with him. A third suggestion was that Raija would tell us that she had made a contract with her husband. According to this deal, if she failed to lose at least three kilograms each week, she had to submit to as much sex as he wanted. The other side of this deal was that if she succeeded in reducing the three kilograms, she had full control over the amount of sex in their marriage.

Of all these suggestions only the first seemed to appeal to Raija. I continued, "Let's suppose that you are indeed able to eventually lose weight with the help of your ability to better control yourself. When you have reached your goal, who in addition to yourself would you thank for your achievement?"

"I would thank her," said Raija promptly referring to her therapist.

"Yes, and what would you thank her for?" I asked.

"For the fact that she helped me regain my self-confidence," she said.

"Who else?" I continued.

"I would thank the nurse who referred me to Virpi."

"What would you thank her for?"

"I went to see her with my mother because we were both very overweight. I go to see her regularly and talk about my diet, exercise, etc. I haven't always followed her advice but she hasn't ever blamed me. When I've been really down, she's been very supportive."

"What about your mother? Has she been of help, too?"

"Yes. As a matter of fact, she came with me today."

"How kind of her. In what other ways has she been of help to you?"

"She has lost 30 kgs of weight over the past six months."

"So she's been an encouraging example to you. Anyone else you'd like to include? What about your children? Have they been of any help to you in losing weight?"

"My younger daughter has recently become concerned about getting fat. She asks questions like 'Will I get fat if I eat this, mom?'"

"Would you say that, in a way, she reminds you to pay attention to your diet?"

"Yes, I guess so."

"What about your husband? You wouldn't want to leave him out. What could you thank him for?"

"At least he's been patient with me. He's never picked on me or anything like that."

"Hasn't he ever asked you to lose weight?"

"Not before I recently explained to him that it is because I am overweight that I don't want to have sex with him."

"Would you say that his being so gentle has been of help to you?"

"Yes, for example, he's taken the children swimming. I have been ashamed to show myself in a bathing suit."

"Fine. Is there still someone who has been of help to you but hasn't been mentioned yet?"

"I have a close woman friend with whom I can talk about anything. She has been an enormous support."

After having scanned Raija's social network and encouraged her to give credit to as many people as possible, I returned once again to the positive future.

"Let's assume that someday you are indeed happy with your weight and both you and your husband are reasonably satisfied with your sex life. What other positive changes do you foresee?"

"I've always avoided places where there are people. I guess I would go out more."

"Anything else?"

"I would be able to go swimming."

"That's right! You'd probably even wear a bikini, wouldn't you?"

"I'd have a different bikini for every day of the week," said Raija laughing.

Before we ended the session someone in the group wanted to take the opportunity to compliment Raija. She said, "You mentioned that you have been afraid of people, but what we have seen today proves the opposite. You have discussed quite candidly with our group (there were some 20 people present) intimate personal questions such as sex and weight. I think that alone proves you to be a courageous person."

About a year later I received a phone call from Virpi. She said that Raija had been pleased with the session, had started losing weight soon afterwards and had eventually managed to lose almost 20 kgs. The therapist felt that there was no longer any need for psychotherapy, but since Raija's weight problem had gone through some ups and downs she continued to visit the nurse for counseling.

Sharing credit for improvement can be used not only to enhance collaboration among professionals but also to help clients develop warmer and more supportive relationships with their families, peers, and other people. For this reason we often encourage our clients to award credit for their improvement not only to those people who seem obviously to deserve it, but also to those who have until now been viewed in a more negative manner. Giving credit to one's "adversaries" for progress achieved is a particularly effective way of conquering former resentments and improving relationships.

The following story illustrates this idea. We had a follow-up workshop with the "Anti-Muiluttaja Association" introduced in the example "The Muiluttaja" in chapter "Fruitful Explanations". During the course of the day we gave the ex-users the task of thinking about how the various significant people in their lives, including family members, friends, and professional helpers, had contributed to their recovery. The participants had no difficulty at all in showing gratitude to their fellow residents, the staff, and their parents, but everyone seemed to have someone in their social network whom they found difficult to thank. Mike, a former addict and pusher, said that he was unable to think of a way to thank a particular police inspector with whom he had been in unpleasant contact numerous times over the years. Mike went on to tell about the inspector he particularly resented. He said, "You know what he told me when I was released after my last nine-day detention? He came to the door as I was leaving and said, 'See you under the bridges, on skid row!' I thought to myself that I'd never bloody well give him the pleasure of seeing me under any bridges!"

"So you could, in fact, thank him for what he said, couldn't you?" said Tapani.

"I see what you mean," said Mike.

We have maintained that giving credit to as many people as possible, even those previously seen as having contributed to the problem rather than its solution, serves to improve relationships and thus to increase the likelihood of further progress. There is, however, another important aspect of sharing credit which deserves attention.

Often, particularly in the case of longstanding problems associated with offensive behavior, many of the people involved become justifiably skeptical about the possibility of any change. This produces an atmosphere of hopelessness which, perhaps because it is experienced as discouraging by the client, may serve to maintain the problem behavior.

The resurrection of optimism in such a situation is easier said than done, as news about progress tends to be discarded as false or meaningless. Here, however, acknowledging the contribution of many people in the person's social network can help those people to become more supportive of change. When one is given credit for a particular positive change one is more likely to see that it has actually happened.

The following example is about a young man who was coached to give credit to various people in his social network for his progress. The aim here was to help others to appreciate his improvement so that he would become considered to be ready for discharge.

A Letter of Gratitude

Pave was a 17-year-old teenager who had been in treatment in the adolescent unit of a psychiatric hospital for nearly two years. He was invited to a session of our ongoing seminar by his designated nurse.

We started the interview by focusing on recent progress. We found that, despite the fact that Pave currently spent most of the time on his ward doing nothing at all, there had been some recent achievements. He had just finished school with relatively good grades, he played occasionally in the hospital's rock and roll band, and in accordance with his rehabilitation plan he had lately completed a two-week trial work period. In addition, Pave had informed his nurse that he seriously intended to get a real job for the coming summer.

We also learned that Pave had been diagnosed as having a borderline personality disorder and that the head physician had recently announced, to Pave's disappointment, that he would need another year of treatment.

"Do you believe that you have made more progress than the staff at the hospital know?" Tapani asked.

"Yes," said Pave.

"What about the head physician, is he aware of your improvement?"

"I doubt it," said Pave, and his nurse agreed.

"Do you think, Pave, that you might be discharged earlier if the staff, and particularly the head physician, could be convinced of your progress?"

"I would think so."

"What would have to happen to convince the staff?" said Tapani directing his question to the nurse.

"He would have to work for the whole of the summer and show true interest in getting himself a profession," she said.

"Well, Pave, do you think you could manage that?" asked Tapani.

"I don't see why not. I worked for two weeks and it went well and I have already decided to find myself a job for the summer," explained Pave.

Ben then said to Pave, "There is something you could do to increase your chances of getting out of the hospital earlier than planned. Are you interested?"

"Yeah," said Pave.

We then explained the idea of awarding credit for progress to as many people as possible and invited Pave to give it a try.

"Who would be the first person on your list to be thanked? How about your nurse?" asked Ben.

"Sure," said Pave.

"We would like you to be more specific. In what way has she helped you?"

"She's encouraged me and she's had faith in me. She's the best nurse on the ward."

We continued in this fashion to look at the contributions made by various people: Pave's mother, his teacher, some of his friends, etc. When we came to the head physician Pave found it difficult to think of a way to thank him, but his nurse came to his rescue. She reported that some time ago Pave had written a letter of complaint to the head physician. He had responded by inviting Pave to come and talk to him in person.

"How kind of him," said Ben. "When you went to talk with him, how did it go?"

"Quite well. He asked me lots of questions and listened to what I had to say."

"How did that feel?"

"Pretty good."

We then recommended that in the near future Pave, with his nurse's assistance, write a letter about his progress, including a word of thanks to all those people who had contributed to his improvement. Both Pave and the nurse agreed to the task and we concluded the session.

We later learned from the staff of the ward that Pave had liked his session with us and that he had even bragged about the experience to some of the other residents on the ward. Pave and his nurse worked out a letter that thanked all the people who had been of help and sent a photocopy of the letter to each of them. Pave found himself a job the next summer as a gardener's assistant. At work he was well liked and in spite of the fact that he was occasionally absent from work without permission he was allowed to keep the job. When he was discharged the following autumn he moved back home to live with his mother and continued his work with the gardener.

We have shown how clients can be coached to thank others for actual or anticipated progress, even those they view in some way as adversaries. The idea of expressing gratitude can be extended beyond people. With a little imagination it is possible to give credit to a variety of things in one's life: ordeals one has gone through in the past, current adverse circumstances, and even the actual problems one is struggling with (see chapter nine, "Problems as Friends").

In the following case, drawn from one of our workshops the client was coached to give credit for his progress not only to his family, friends, and professional helpers, but also to his current problem.

Overcoming Bankruptcy

Niko was a businessman in his late forties who had formerly run a successful company selling car parts. His business had earned him and his family an affluent lifestyle. They lived in a nice house and the two sons, 12-year-old Ilpo and eight-year-old Simo each were both active in sports. In his time Niko had been successful at sports and now both his sons were following in his footsteps.

For the past two years Niko had suffered insurmountable problems with his company. In spite of considerable financial assistance from his parents, the company had finally gone bankrupt. He had been indicted for financial wrongdoing and a lawsuit had been filed against him. On top of this, the local newspapers treated his case in a far from kindly manner. Niko became desperate. He turned sullen and begun to drink excessively. One day he drove when he was drunk with the result that he wrecked his car and barely saved his skin. He was arrested and convicted; his license was revoked for several years.

The fact that Niko eventually won the lawsuit filed against him did not make things any better. He was now unemployed and had personal responsibility for huge loans. Elaine, Niko's wife, had started to talk about divorce, and finally Niko agreed to be admitted to a psychiatric hospital for crisis treatment.

The social worker in the hospital invited Niko and his

family to the consultation. We started the interview by discussing a positive view of the future. In this fantasy Niko had overcome his problems and the family's economic situation was once more relatively stable. The children were doing well at school and succeeding in motocross competitions. Elaine had completed her studies and now had a stable job. Niko was no longer drinking to excess and had found himself a job in his own field, not as an entrepreneur, but as an employee in someone else's company.

We then took up the subject of progress and found that much improvement had already taken place. Niko was no longer unapproachable; he had become open and willing to talk about his problems. His elder son had noticed that Niko had begun to smile again, and the social worker reported that his mood had changed for the better. Elaine had recently enrolled in a correspondence course at a business college. After lengthy conversations with his bank manager, Niko had worked out a schedule for reducing his heavy debts.

We then asked Niko to whom he would like to give credit for his progress besides himself. He readily thanked his wife and his children for their patience and their support and thanked the staff of the hospital, particularly the social worker. We asked him if he was grateful to any of his friends. He said, "This whole thing has been a kind of friendship test which has helped me to tell real friends from people who are just there for what they can get. I've realized that I do have a few real friends and they have been of enormous help."

Ben said, "We've made optimistic fantasies about the future and we've been talking about the progress already made. However, we all know that many obstacles still lie ahead."

"We are well aware of that," said Elaine, and Niko nodded in agreement.

"What we could do now is to make a list of some of the

challenges you're going to have to deal with in the future," said Ben.

Niko and Elaine readily agreed and told us that in the near future their family would have to become accustomed to living with a smaller income than before, that Niko needed to find a job and get used to the idea of working for someone else. They would both have to learn to live with the fact that for many years a good deal of their income would be spent on reducing Niko's debts.

"What about earning back your dignity?" asked Tapani. "Has your reputation suffered as a result of what has happened and do you need to do something about it?"

"You're right and that's the really tough part," admitted Niko.

"We like to say," continued Ben, "that the pride in overcoming a problem should overshadow the shame of having had it. Do you agree?"

"I sure do," said Niko.

We explained to Niko that in terms of overcoming his future obstacles he might benefit from finding something to thank his problem for. We first asked him to give his current ordeal a nickname. He discussed for a while with his wife and then decided to call it "Hope." We then suggested that within a few days the social worker should meet Niko and Elaine at the hospital. At this meeting the two of them were to think of five quotations epitomizing what "Hope" had taught them. All parties agreed to this suggestion and we closed the session.

A few weeks later we called the social worker to find out what had happened. She told us that soon after the consultation she had arranged a meeting with Niko and Elaine and without any input from her they had come up with ten quotations and maxims. Niko made two posters of them and had them framed. When he left the hospital a little while later he took one of the posters with him and made a gift of the other to the staff. He had begun searching for a job in another town and his family was thinking about moving. Niko's gift still hangs on the wall of the psychiatric ward, raising curiosity and bringing hope to new patients.

The resolution of problems appears to be a social process which the various people involved can either jeopardize or encourage. Acknowledging as many people as possible as having done their share in promoting progress is an effective antidote to blame and a kindly invitation for those involved to join the side advocating positive change.

9

PROBLEMS AS FRIENDS

It is told that once upon a time in China there lived a poor old man who had only one son and a horse. One cold autumn day his horse broke loose and galloped away into the mountains. The villagers came to him and said, "Oh you poor old man, what misfortune has come your way. We came to say that we all feel sorry for you." But the old man said, "Don't feel sorry for me. You never can tell whether what happens to you is fortune or misfortune."

Some time later the old man's horse returned accompanied by ten of the most magnificent wild horses. The villagers came to him and said, "Oh you lucky man, what good fortune has come your way. We came to say we all feel happy for you." But the old man said, "Don't feel happy for me. You never can tell whether what happens to you is fortune or misfortune."

The old man's son started to tame the wild horses. Everything went well until one day he was thrown by one of the wild horses and broke his leg. The villagers came to him and said, "Oh you poor man, what misfortune has come your way. We came to say we all feel sorry for you." But the old man said, "Don't feel sorry for me. You never can tell whether what happens to you is fortune or misfortune."

Some weeks went by and a fierce war broke out in China. All young men were called to arms but the old man's son could not go because he lay in bed with his broken leg . . .

We have a saying in Finland: "However much there is that is bad, there is always some good in it." In addition to bringing suffering, hardships and times of trouble also have positive consequences. Even extreme tragedies, such as the untimely death of a child, can be seen years later as an experience that brought about something valuable, such as an increased sensitivity to the suffering of others.

An insight into the brighter side of a current predicament makes it easier to endure. When problems are seen in a positive light, people become more creative in solving them. In the case of longstanding problems, it often appears that people are better able to make progress only after they realize that in addition to pain their problem has also given them something valuable.

In suggesting that clients consider the possible positive consequences of their situation it is important to remember that this is not always easy to do when the problems are acute. For example, suggesting to people who have recently experienced loss that they look at the positive side may be considered offensive. The realization that there is very often a brighter side to our problems tends to come later, when we are able to look back and put things into a different perspective.

The following vignette by Tapani describes a supervision session at a psychiatric hospital. The client is coached to consider the positive side of her misfortune as Tapani invites her to look back on her current circumstances from the far distant future.

Wisdom for the Grandchildren

I conducted a consultation session in the adolescent inpatient unit of a psychiatric hospital. The client invited to the group that day was Siru, a 15-year-old girl who had been a patient on the ward for a few months.

I started the session by asking about Siru's progress and found that she had taken major steps toward her recovery. For example, she had done particularly well at the hospital school. She had also recently spent her first weekend at home with her mother and all had gone well.

I interviewed Siru, focusing on her progress instead of problems. This approach did not appear to be sufficient for the staff and they politely indicated that I should also address some of the problems.

I went along with this proposal. I said to Siru, "It appears that you've made much progress, but how did you come to be here in the first place?"

"I'm here because I went crazy," she said in a matter-of-fact way.

"And what made you go crazy?" I continued.

"My father killed himself and I couldn't take it."

One of the nurses explained that Siru's father had been an alcoholic for many years and that one day when he had been heavily drunk he had taken his life. We talked for some time about what had happened and how, with the help of the hospital, Siru had eventually been able to cope with the tragedy.

Towards the end of the meeting I said, "You have gone through a very rough period in your life and what has happened has undoubtedly had a great impact on you. It may be impossible to foresee what the effects will be in the long run, but let's imagine that some time in the far distant future you are a grandmother with an adult daughter and a teenage granddaughter. You have told your daughter about your father's suicide and about the time you spent in a mental hospital. Your daughter, in turn, has told your story to her daughter. Your story will serve as a teaching story. It will be wisdom that is of value not only to your daughter but also to your granddaughter. What do you imagine that wisdom might be?"

After a moment of silence Siru said, "First, I've realized that it is possible to survive even the most terrible things." She paused and then continued, "Second, I used to be the kind of person who kept my thoughts to myself. That wasn't good. Here at the hospital I've learned that talking helps."

Problems teach us about life and they bring about personal growth, but sometimes they can have an even more fascinating quality: they actually help to solve other problems. This was vividly brought home to us by the case of a young man who, after attempting suicide, appeared to have solved a problem that had been a burden to him for years. The story is told by Ben.

The Curative Suicide Attempt

I received a phone call from a woman who was worried about Mikko, her nephew, and wanted to make him an appointment for a consultation. She told me that Mikko was a high school student who had been doing fine until about a month ago when without any warning he made an attempt to kill himself by taking an overdose of sleeping pills. He had been rushed to hospital, kept there for the night, and allowed home the following day. Mikko's suicide attempt had come as a terrible shock to everyone in the family.

During the telephone conversation I also learned that some months prior to his suicide attempt Mikko had been told that the man he knew as his father was in fact his stepfather. After asking for and obtaining information about his biological father, he had called him and they had agreed to meet. The encounter had been brief; it had appeared to Mikko that his real father was not interested in maintaining further contact.

This series of events, added to the fact that Mikko was heavily burdened by his high school studies, was thought by the family to have triggered the suicide attempt.

A few days later Mikko was in my office. In a confident and open manner he explained how he was presently busy with his studies and he also spoke about his girlfriend, with whom he had been going steady for about a year. The events that had occurred some weeks previously seemed to belong to the past.

I gave Mikko a summary of my conversation with his aunt and asked him about the suicide attempt. He candidly told me the details of the night when he took the overdose. I got the impression that he had really meant to take his life even though the quantity of tranquilizers he had swallowed was insufficient to kill him.

He also told me about the recent meeting and explained that, even though it was true that his real father was not interested in maintaining further contact, it was not the reason for his suicide attempt.

I was interested in hearing Mikko's own explanation and asked him if he wanted to tell me. He told me that when he was in his first few years at primary school he used to have a good friend, Jolle. Mikko and Jolle were almost glued to each other. One day, for no apparent reason, Jolle abandoned Mikko and started to play with the other boys instead. This incident broke Mikko's heart. He came to believe that there must be something wrong with him even if he could not figure out what it was.

Mikko never spoke about his misery to anyone and he secretly started to harbor thoughts of self-reproach and suicide. The memory of his rejection and the plans for killing himself had stayed with Mikko throughout the years. According to him, the suicide attempt was not precipitated by his current circumstances as the family seemed to think, but was the completion of a private plan he had kept hidden for years.

When Mikko had finished his story I asked, "What now, after your suicide attempt? Have you spoken about these things to your family?"

"I have spoken with my father more than ever."

"So, he now knows all about Jolle and the suicidal thoughts that you used to have but kept secret from everyone?"

"Yes."

Mikko explained that besides speaking with his stepfather he had also talked with his mother and his girlfriend about many things he had previously kept inside. It appeared that in some way his suicide attempt had acted as a rite of passage: a formerly reserved young man who used to conceal his tormenting thoughts and feelings had become able to open up his heart to those close to him.

"This may seem odd to you, Mikko," I said, "but in a sense we could say that these events – your overdose and its aftermath – have changed you. You used to keep important thoughts and feelings inside yourself but your suicide attempt has helped you to somehow unlock your ability to talk. After recovering from your overdose you spoke of your intentions and while doing this you realized that you could actually talk about anything. The problem of keeping things to yourself seems to have dissolved as you now feel able to say to others whatever it is you need to tell them. What do you think? Is this correct?"

"Yes, it's true," said Mikko.

We talked for a while about how after the suicide attempt Mikko had in many ways become more mature as a person. I then explained to him how I was now in a slightly complicated situation:

"Your family may think that you need psychotherapy and now it appears that your suicide attempt, in a sense, cured you. How would your parents react to this idea?"

"Oh, I think they would agree. I have spoken with them so much lately."

"What about your aunt? If you were to explain this to her would she feel that I'm not taking your case seriously enough?"

"I can explain to her. I think she would understand, too."

I said that in the light of what had transpired during the session it appeared to me that there was probably no need for psychotherapy. I thanked Mikko for an interesting discussion and walked him to the door. As he was leaving I said he knew my number if he ever needed my help and wished him good luck with his studies.

It was only after the session that I began to have second thoughts. Was my view that Mikko's suicide attempt had been a self-cure appropriate or had I simply been too eager to make the therapy brief? I suspected that many of my colleagues would disapprove, but somehow I felt I had done the right thing.

I followed up on this case after a month and then again after a year. I learned that Mikko's parents had at first been doubtful about my decision not to recommend further therapy. They had, however, gradually become more confident that it was the right decision, as they observed that Mikko did well in his studies, had many friends, and appeared, in mother's words, to be a sunny boy.

We thought a lot about Mikko's case as it somehow seemed to epitomize the idea that problems are sometimes solutions. Since then we have used the story on a number of occasions to invite other clients to think about their problems in somewhat similar fashion. The following story, which is drawn from a training seminar, serves as an example.

You As Well?

A psychiatrist brought Kurt, a middle aged man, in for a consultation session. He had been suffering from anxiety attacks in social situations. Kurt had been very successful both in his work and in his private life. He was well-known in his local community as an active participant in a variety of municipal activities.

Some months previously Kurt's success story had taken a U-turn because of his devastating anxiety problem. He told us that he had suffered from anxiety in social situations since his school years. He had been so ashamed of this "weakness" that he had controlled it by sheer willpower and never spoken about it to anyone. His willpower had time and again enabled him to overcome his fear of performing in public until, one day, the problem had defeated him. He was forced to leave in the middle of an important meeting because his anxiety had become unbearable.

Kurt was convinced that everyone in the meeting had noticed his problem. Since then he had been unable to take part in any social situations or attend any meetings and had remained at home, becoming increasingly depressed about his predicament.

Finally Kurt opened up and candidly revealed his problem first to his wife and then to his children. The family members were astonished, as they had no suspicion of his difficulties. His wife turned to a psychologist friend of hers, who met them both and suggested that Kurt see a psychiatrist. Kurt consulted a psychiatrist, who decided to invite him to a consultation at our training center.

As Kurt told us his story, we were vividly reminded of what had happened to Mikko. We summarized Mikko's story for Kurt and then asked him, "Could it be that in your case the same kind of thing has happened? Your problem began to solve itself as you began to be more open about it?"

"Yes," he said, "that is exactly what has happened and now I understand that talking about it has been of enormous help to me. First I told my wife and children about it, then the psychologist, then this psychiatrist, and finally this whole crowd!" This provoked a ripple of laughter in the training group.

"So in a way we could say that your recent suffering hasn't been in vain. The fact that your problem became worse helped you to solve it altogether."

Kurt agreed, "I think that's true!"

"Well, how do you feel now that the problem is over?" asked Tapani with a smile.

Kurt was astonished by this remark but he quickly recovered, smiled back and said, "Very good indeed."

As the session continued Kurt became convinced that he might indeed have overcome his problem by becoming more open about it. At the end of the session he took us by surprise by giving a brief but impressive speech about how problems can be helpful to us if only we have the courage to face them. Finally, as Kurt was getting ready to leave he wished us all the best and recommended that we all go through a similar depression sometime in our life. "That'll make you even better therapists!" he said. The group, amused by Kurt's enthusiasm, wished him the best of luck. We learned later from his psychiatrist that Kurt had been appreciative of the session and was currently doing fine.

In our experience, suggesting to clients the idea that a problem has been in some way helpful or useful is best done in a delicate manner, preferably by telling a story. The following case, also drawn from our training seminar, is another example of suggesting the idea that problems can be solutions by relating the experiences of former clients.

Teaching Illness

Ismo, a manager in his late forties, was invited in for a consultation session by a general practitioner who attended our training seminar. Ismo had visited his physician regularly once a fortnight for the past few months.

We learned that Ismo had been suffering from what had been diagnosed as panic attacks for over a year. Apparently the problem had been precipitated by Ismo being made responsible for the reorganization of the company he worked for, a process which involved laying off dozens of former employees.

Ismo's problem had been so intense that he had been unable to go to work for more than six months. His staying at home all day had led to tensions within the family.

Ismo described his problem as sudden and unpredictable attacks of palpitation that made him believe that his heart was about to stop altogether. Several times while driving he had pulled over to the side of the road and called for an ambulance. Innumerable ECG recordings had been made but none of them had shown anything to be wrong. During the past year Ismo had made very frequent visits to the Accident and Emergency Department at his local hospital.

"Has there been recent progress?" asked Tapani.

"What would you say?" said Ismo to his physician.

"Yes, there has been major progress," said the physician. He explained that Ismo was now back at work, had stopped visiting the Accident and Emergency Department, and had endured some months since requesting an ECG be taken. Ismo himself added that by driving alone a distance of 40 kilometers to the consultation he had taken another major step in his recovery. This was indeed a major achievement, since up until now he had been avoiding driving and had only dared to drive distances of a few kilometers from his home town.

"Well, do you think your problem might be over?" asked Tapani.

"It's much better, but it's very difficult for me to believe it's really over," said Ismo.

"There is, of course, the possibility that you will have further attacks, but let's just suppose that the problem is over and done with," said Tapani.

At this point Ben asked the group, "Do you know what is meant by the term 'teaching hospital'?"

After having received the expected answer to this question, Ben continued, "That's right, but do you know what is meant by the term 'teaching illness'?"

No one knew the meaning of this baffling concept. "It's an illness that teaches you something valuable about life," explained Ben and in order to make his point continued by briefly relating the stories of Mikko and Kurt.

"Let's suppose, Ismo," said Tapani, "that your problem has in fact been a teaching illness. In that case what could it be that you've gained from having had this problem?"

Ismo reflected on the question but was unable immediately to come up with anything concrete. In order to assist him we asked more specific questions, inviting him to consider whether he had noticed any improvements in his own personal growth, physical health, family relationships, work, spiritual life, friendships, hobbies, etc.

It turned out that many positive consequences had followed from Ismo's problem. He had reduced his alcohol consumption, improved his diet and increased his sporting activities. He had become closer than ever to his wife and had found more time to play with their child. He had become more sympathetic to other people with similar problems. For example, he had recently had a lengthy conversation with an employee who was troubled by a stomach ulcer. Ismo also disclosed that the problem had renewed his spirituality. He had begun to read religious literature and had entered into conversations with his wife and some of his close friends about religious questions.

"If, indeed, your problem has been a teaching illness, it looks like it has already accomplished its purpose," said Tapani and continued with a twinkle in his eye, "Well, how do you feel now that you're cured?"

Ismo laughed with both relief and disbelief. We then recommended that he return to the employee with the stomach ulcer and tell him how in his own case the problem had been a teaching illness. We advised him to encourage the employee to explore his circumstances and see whether his stomach ulcer problem was also a teaching illness. Ismo accepted this task and we drew the session to a close.

About a month after the consultation we heard from Ismo's physician that the attacks had ceased. Ismo had said to him, "I guess I left the problem there."

To help people think constructively about their difficulties it is often useful to invite them to come up with a name or even a nickname to refer to their problems. It is difficult to think positively about one's "borderline personality" but once problems are named more personally it becomes far easier to recognize the beneficial consequences that have already come about and imagine those which may eventually occur.

The following example is drawn from a workshop we conducted at Bechterew Institute, in Leningrad, at which the client is invited to give a nickname to his problem. This new name is then used in helping him to view his problem in a more positive light.

Ivanushka

Lenit, a psychiatrist from the neurosis department of the hospital, had invited Igor and Natasha, a young couple in their early thirties, for a demonstration interview. Lenit, who had decided to record the interview on video, told us from behind his camera that he had met with Igor a few times but that this was the first time Natasha had been invited along.

Tapani directed his first question to Lenit, "Suppose that one day your video, 'The story of Igor and Natasha,' is completed. What will it be? A tragedy, a comedy, or a love story? Or could it perhaps be an educational video?"

Lenit said that he would like his film to become an educational video.

Tapani directed the following question to the audience, "I'd be interested to hear if you have any fantasies about what the film would teach. First of all, how do you imagine the film would end?"

Igor interrupted to explain that his problem was so complex that it was impossible to imagine any final scene which could demonstrate that the problem was over. He asked for permission to explain to all of us what his problem was. He then stood up and gave a five-minute description of his problem. From the simultaneous translation we gathered that Igor had experienced a crisis. He had felt lonely and become alienated from other people. He had done a lot of thinking and suffered from the feeling that he had lost contact with his own thoughts.

"Would you say your husband gave an accurate account of his problem?" Ben asked Natasha.

"Yes, he explained the problem exactly as it is," said Natasha, who appeared proud of her husband.

"What we would like the two of you to do now," said Tapani, "is to give this problem a name so it will be easier for us to talk about it. We would like you to give it a pleasant name because problems can have nicknames just like people. Try to find a nickname for the problem."

Igor and Natasha talked to each other for a few moments and Igor then said that they would like to suggest the name "Ivan." An elderly Russian woman in the audience suggested that the couple call the problem "Ivanushka," which is the diminutive form of the name Ivan. They gladly approved.

"Let's imagine," Tapani continued, "that one day in the future we meet somewhere, say at the marketplace in Helsinki. We are sipping coffee together in the sun with the two of you. We talk for a while and discover that you are both very happy. We ask you about Ivanushka. What do you say?"

"We say that we haven't seen him for a long, long time," said Igor. Natasha smiled.

"What else do you tell us? Would you proudly introduce us to all your six children?" joked Tapani.

"Heavens no!" said Natasha. "One or two at the most."

"We then ask you the following question," continued Tapani. "Looking back, could you say that Ivanushka was in some way useful to you?"

Here Lenit entered the discussion and said that he had observed that Natasha and Igor had become closer to each other in the face of Igor's current problems. They agreed and said that they had learned to understand one another better. They also told us that they had recently had many long and penetrating philosophical discussions.

Tapani turned to Igor and said, "Let us imagine that

some time in the future you decide to throw a party to celebrate the fact that Ivanushka has been gone for a long time. You invite your wife and perhaps some friends. Do you also invite Lenit, your doctor?"

"Yes, of course," said Igor.

"What about your old friend Ivanushka? Would you consider inviting him, too?" said Tapani and continued, "You may think right now that Ivanushka is a nuisance in your life, but in the future you may see him differently. Ivanushka may then seem like a teacher who came into your life to show you something valuable. How would you feel about inviting him?"

"Not only would I invite him, but I would seat him at the head of the table," said Igor.

"Do you think that Ivanushka has actually been a philosophy teacher?" asked Ben and went on to explain, "Not the kind of philosophy teacher who teaches you what the books say, but a practical philosophy teacher who puts you through ordeals and teaches you by experiment. Practical philosophy teachers are often quite annoying but we tend to feel grateful towards them later. Does this make any sense? Are you by nature a philosopher, Igor?"

"I can answer that question," said Natasha. "Yes, Igor is very much a philosopher. People often come to our house to discuss things with him. He is very good at that."

"In that case, could it perhaps be that Igor used to have his head in the clouds and Ivanushka came along to teach him to keep his feet on the ground?" asked Ben playfully.

Igor smiled and Natasha said, "It could well be." We then brought the session to an end by suggesting to Lenit that he might consider titling his video "Ivanushka."

The following example, provided by Ben, illustrates the use of the idea of the problem being a friend in the case of a child. Here, as in so many other cases, it is difficult to know for certain what role the conversation played in the subsequent recovery, but it is exciting and surely gratifying to think that it was helpful.

The Sleeper

Jouni was a 10-year-old boy with a peculiar problem that prevented him from attending school. For the past three months he had been sleeping all day and all night. He came to the table for meals but after he had finishing he immediately went back to bed. Before the sleeping problem began Jouni had suffered from a painful neck, which medical doctors had been unable to treat adequately. A number of naturopathic healers had also tried, to no avail. Finally, the parents had taken Jouni to see an osteopath who, according to the family, had quickly cured Jouni's neck pain with just a few twists. Unfortunately, right after recovering from his painful neck Jouni had acquired his current sleeping problem.

Jouni, who seemed to be a intelligent boy, was quite alert when he came in with his family for consultation. Only a quarter of an hour into the session he started to complain about sleepiness and asked for permission to go to sleep. I told him to go ahead and he curled up on the sofa beside his father.

I continued to talk with his parents and I learned that during the past few weeks there had been only meager progress. Jouni had stayed awake at times for as long as half an hour. I observed Jouni as he was lying on the sofa and got the impression that he was not sleeping in the physiological sense of the word but that he was just dozing. I shared this observation with the parents and they said that the doctors who had recorded his brain waves (EEG) at a child psychiatric hospital had said the same thing. Since I suspected that Jouni was able to hear our discussion I decided to continue as if he was actively listening.

"What is Jouni good at?" I asked.

"He is good at drawing comic strips," said father. "He draws detailed picture stories that are sometimes several pages long."

"That's wonderful," I said. "Perhaps we could think of a

way he can use his talent to help himself. Let me tell you what little I know about the North American Indians. I have heard that there are tribes where every now and then a person starts to behave in a peculiar way. This person then goes off into the mountains to live in solitude. They say that the person is "a seeker of vision" and that he is going through a painful transformation process from being an ordinary tribesman to becoming a healer and a knower of wisdom. He has to go through all kinds of hardships, and when he finally returns to his village he is respected as a person who is capable of helping others. Would it be possible to think that Jouni is going through something like this?"

"This is very interesting," said mother. "When I was in my teens I became very ill. My legs became so weak that I couldn't walk and the doctors said that I had a progressive muscle disease. Finally they surgically removed my thymus gland and after that operation I quickly recovered."

"Do you think your illness was an ordeal that helped you in some way?" I asked, "For example, did it make you better at understanding other people with problems or something like that?"

"Yes. As a matter of fact, many of my friends turn to me for help when they have problems."

"So it is not impossible for you to think that Jouni's problem could be some kind of rite of passage that will make him grow and perhaps become helpful to others in the future."

I then suggested that this view could be used in helping Jouni. Our conversation led to a plan that father would ask Jouni to work with him in putting together a comic strip on this theme. We thought of a few examples, one of which was the story of a space warrior who is weakened by dangerous rays but who when he has recovered finds that he is endowed with the power of giving strength to others. We then ended the session. Jouni did not wake up so his father had to carry him to the car.

A few weeks after the session I received a phone call from the mother. She said that there had been a dramatic change the previous week. Jouni had been taken by his parents to receive treatment from a "zone therapist" specializing in foot massage. She had diagnosed the problem as "pneumonia" and given an appropriate massage. The next day Jouni's problem had gone and since then he had attended school, done his chores and everything was back to normal. I called the mother after a year and she informed me that there had been no further problems.

There are problems in all societies that are considered shameful to have or to not be able to cope with in the expected way. The mechanisms responsible for perpetuating problems are undoubtedly manifold, but it is certain that both shame and the fear of losing face play pivotal roles in preserving problems and often making them worse.

The feeling of being regarded as abnormal or inadequate by those whom one is close to prevents people from facing problems and restrains the creativity which might lead to the discovery of solutions. Seeing problems as learning opportunities, passages of growth, or hardships with an important message, helps in the replacement of shame with dignity.

10

TEACHING AND TRAINING

Practice what you preach.

In recent years a new resource-oriented philosophy of approaching human problems has emerged in the field of psychotherapy. This philosophy builds upon openness and cooperation focusing on what is positive – on strengths, progress, and solutions. The application of this philosophy is not restricted to psychotherapy; it appears to be relevant across the entire spectrum of the helping services.

In line with this view, when we started our first training seminar we decided to invite applications not only from physicians, psychologists, social workers and psychiatric nurses, but also from other people employed within the human services. As a result of this policy our training groups are usually made up of individuals representing a rich variety of backgrounds. This has been good as it has given us the opportunity to consult with clients representing an equally rich variety of problems; also, our trainees have had a chance to work closely with professionals and people with whom they would ordinarily have little or no contact. In their feedback our trainees have repeatedly acknowledged the usefulness of having had the opportunity to work "across the borders."

We believe that there are at least four ways of gaining mastery of an art. Reading about it can be helpful, listening to someone talk about it is better, observing somebody actually do it surpasses both of these, but getting to practice it oneself is the road to success.

Our training emphasizes the importance of "hands on" work to the extent that we do not use the limited time available to review relevant literature. We expect that if we ask our trainees to read and discuss books they would learn to read and discuss books.

Professional books and articles are of course a valuable source of inspiration and understanding. They are particularly so when read out of a desire to learn more rather than because of an obligation to study. To encourage our trainees to explore literature on their own we do not have a specified list of books or articles for them to read. We count on the fact that both their confusion and their innate curiosity motivate them. When they begin, most trainees are familiar with some of the relevant literature and during training all of them read more.

Some of our trainees have accurately remarked that many of the ideas presented in our training can also be found in nonprofessional literature. For example, one of our trainees discovered that many of the ideas of solution talk also appear in the literature on optimism and positive thinking (e.g., McGinnis, 1990).

Our primary method of teaching is demonstration, conducting sessions with "real" clients. When this is not feasible we use other procedures: telling stories as we have done in this book; asking trainees to discuss their previous successes; allowing trainees to generate solutions for their personal problems; and inviting trainees to discuss their own ongoing cases with the group. All these approaches serve to encourage rediscovery of useful ideas and discovery of new ones. In discussing problems presented by our trainees we follow the rule "never argue with the client." We offer several suggestions instead of just one and let our trainees decide for themselves which of the recommendations, if any, appear useful to them.

Soon after the completion of our first training seminar we discovered that many of our former trainees had lost much of their enthusiasm for their newly acquired ideas. A good number of them complained that, even though they continued to receive plenty of support from their fellow trainees, they were challenged by their colleagues, by associates and managers at their places of work, and even by their own family members. They experienced significant resistance to all their efforts to implement changes in the routines with which problems were handled.

We realized that we had failed to consider the environment in which our trainees worked and that we had inadvertently contributed to the quite normal tension between those who are in external training and those who are not. We had unwittingly encouraged the impression that our trainees were faced with resistance to change, a notion which was in marked contrast to the ideas we professed.

As we began to look for ways to help our trainees achieve better collaboration at their places of work, we realized that many of the approaches we readily used with clients were quite appropriate, especially the idea of sharing credit. We invited our trainees to think of the ways in which the people they worked with, particularly those with whom they frequently disagreed, may have contributed to their acquisition of new ideas. We then encouraged our trainees to share these thoughts with their colleagues.

We also encouraged our trainees to offer their team members the opportunity of taking part in our training for a day. This offer was well received and since that time we have regularly had one or two extra members sitting in on our sessions. When asked to share their impressions with us, these visitors have said without exception that they found the experience interesting and that they now understood their colleagues much better.

Our positive experience with invited visitors encouraged us to experiment with moving our entire training sessions, often involving 20 or more people, into our trainees' working places. The idea of such an "ambulatory school" is to give members of the staff who work in these places the opportunity to observe and become acquainted with our approach.

Over the years we have visited a wide variety of locations, such as psychiatric wards, mental health centers, residential treatment homes for children, child guidance centers, and ordinary schools. On one occasion we received an invitation from an occupational physician to visit a coal power plant, where our training group met a team of blue-collar workers and their manager and helped them in finding solutions to a longstanding confidentiality crisis.

When training groups are made up of professionals working for a specific organization or when they come from a specified region, the idea of "ambulatory school" is particularly appropriate. For example, when we had the opportunity to teach a group of special teachers all employed by the same town, the group decided to meet each time at a different school; this allowed us to invite interested regular teachers to take part in the sessions. In another town the departments of health care and social services collaborated to sponsor the provision of training in solution-oriented working methods for their staff. We started with an afternoon workshop open to all those who were interested and continued by conducting a dozen small group sessions at various localities in the community.

Early on in our training we entertained the idea of establishing an educational program in brief therapy, which would eventually lead to a diploma and national accreditation. For this purpose we extended our initial one-year training program to include an optional second year which was composed of supervision sessions with us and small group sessions in which the trainees worked by themselves. These small groups each had three to five members and they held weekly sessions with clients at members' places of work. At the monthly supervision sessions the groups had an opportunity to discuss their cases with us.

We soon learned that trainees enjoyed working in small groups with clients. At the monthly supervision sessions they occasionally asked us about difficulties they had encountered but mostly they told us of their accomplishments. Many of them remarked that working in small groups without our dominating presence was so rewarding that they should have been given the opportunity to work that way much earlier in the training.

In designing our next training course we took notice of these opinions and arranged for trainees to begin working on their own in small groups as soon as they were halfway through the year. We found that in spite of initial apprehensions train-ees quickly grew to appreciate working with clients in small groups.

The use of small groups is now an integral element of our training and we usually form them quite early on. Working as a team in small groups appears to be gratifying. A good propor-tion of the small groups that have assembled over the years in different parts of Finland have not only continued to meet but have also begun to communicate their know-how to other pro-fessionals.

Our first programs were founded on the traditional belief that in order to produce results training had to last "long enough." According to Finnish national standards three years of training is required for a therapist to be eligible for the regis-ter of state-accredited therapists. We were at odds with this doctrine since we felt that a training for one academic year coupled with further supervision and working in small groups was quite enough.

Over the years we have experimented with training pro-grams of various lengths and at closing ceremonies we have often discussed with our trainees the question of what is an adequate duration for a training program. Interestingly, re-gardless of the duration of the training they attended, most trainees seem to feel that the duration of their particular train-ing was just right. For example, many of those whose training with us lasted for a whole academic year said that more would have been redundant and less would have been inadequate. Likewise, the majority of those who attended a course consist-ing of six full days spread over a period of three months with the same amount of additional work in small groups agreed with a psychologist who said, "A day less would have been too little and a day more would have been too much. There is enough to digest for a long time."

We have gradually become convinced that it is not necessary for training to last a long time in order to be effective. It ap-pears to us that the belief that long training is preferable to brief training is just as ill-founded as the conventional belief that long-term therapy is better than brief therapy. It is most likely that beliefs about what constitutes an appropriate length of training are to a great degree self-fulfilling prophesies. When we are convinced that it takes at least three years to learn a particular approach, we tend to organize our training in ways which support this belief. On the other hand, when we believe that our ideas can be learned in a significantly briefer period of time, we are likely to arrange training so that this can become true.

There are people who because of geographical, economical, or time constraints cannot undertake regular training. Some years ago we established an ongoing open seminar we call "the inspiration day," which is able to accommodate people with special needs. We hold a whole day workshop regularly once a fortnight but there is no training program with a beginning and an end. Participants decide for themselves the number of times they wish to participate and they pay only for the days they are present. The workshop is always held at the same location in a space large enough to accommodate up to several dozen people. Like our other training formats, the open seminar primarily consists of consultation sessions with clients who are invited by the participants.

Some people have regularly attended the open seminar but several have come just once to observe. Many of the participants view "the inspiration day" not as a training seminar but as an opportunity to work with others in boosting their ability to pay attention to positive aspects of apparently pessimistic situations. Some organizations have reserved a permanent seat at the seminar and organized a rotation system among their staffs, so that on each seminar day we have a different representative from that organization.

The open seminar is not only for professionals working within the helping services but also for anyone interested in learning about solution-oriented approaches, so we call it "the open university." In accordance with the open-door policy, on a number of occasions we have invited our clients to join the group as participants in subsequent sessions. We always start sessions by asking participants to introduce themselves by name and occupation; it is at this point that our clients discover that in addition to professionals, there are also college students, volunteers from various organizations, and sometimes even former clients present at the session. This diversity of participants has never been a problem; in fact, most clients seem pleased by the opportunity to consult such a varied group of people. Sometimes when there are previous clients present, current clients ask them, "Well, how was it for you?"

Our experience of including nonprofessionals in our seminars has encouraged us to spread the ideas of solution talk to a wider audience. More and more often when we visit schools, residential homes, and other institutions our audience consists not only of staff but also of clients, family members, and other interested professionals. We have also had a number of opportunities to talk to large audiences, where the majority of people present have been nonprofessionals.

It appears to us that the kind of ideas we have referred to as solution talk in this book are not exclusive and that they do not sit well with the idea that some people are experts while some are not. These ideas pertain to common sense and can be put to work not only by professionals but also by anyone who is facing problems.

We like to think of solution talk as not a system of therapy with students, teachers, and high priests, but as a quality of conversation. Respect, optimism, kindness and humor are not private property – they belong to everyone.

There is a film by the well-known pair of Danish comedians, Fyrtarnet and Bivogen (known in English speaking countries as Long and Short), where Long comes to Short's house and sees him bustling about in the midst of a bewildering array of chemical equipment.

Long asks Short, "What on earth are you doing?"

"I'm inventing gunpowder," says Short determinedly.

"But my dear Short, gunpowder has already been invented," says Long.

"Never mind," says Short, "I'll invent more!"

This story is pertinent to us not only because one of us is taller than the other but also because we share the belief that, working within the field of human problems, it is useful to maintain the illusion that we are constantly inventing something new. In our hearts we know full well that we are just reinventing the wheel, that our discoveries have been invented many times before, and that they will be invented again and again.

REFERENCES

American Psychiatric Association (1987). *Diagnostic and statistical manual of mental disorders*, (3rd ed., revised) (DSM-III-R). Washington, DC: Author.

Anderson, H., & Goolishian, H. (1988). Human systems as linguistic systems: Preliminary and evolving ideas about the implications on clinical theory. *Family Process, 27*(4):371–393.

Boscolo, L., Cecchin, G., Hoffman, L., & Penn, P. (1988). *Milan systemic family therapy: Conversations in theory and practice*. New York: Basic Books.

Boyd, W.R. (1987). Promoting therapeutic movement through the use of ambiguous function assinments. In S.R. Lankton (Ed.), *Ericksonian Monographs, No 2: Central themes in Ericksonian therapy*. New York: Brunner/Mazel.

de Shazer, S. (1985). *Keys to solution in brief therapy*. New York: Norton.

de Shazer, S. (1988). *Clues: Investigating solutions in brief therapy*. New York: Norton.

de Shazer, S. (1991). *Putting difference to work*. New York: Norton.

de Shazer, S., Berg, I.K., Lipchik, E., Nunnally, E., Molnar, A., Gingerich, W.C., & Weiner-Davis, M. (1986). Brief therapy: Focused solution development. *Family Process, 25*:207–221.

Efran, J., & Heffner K. (1991). Change the name and you change the game. *Journal of Strategic and Systemic Therapies, 10*(1):50–65.

Epston, D. (1990). Collected papers. Adelaide, South Australia: Dulwich Centre Publications.

Farrelly, F., & Brandsma, J. (1974). *Provocative therapy*. Cupertino, CA: Meta.

Fisch, R., Weakland, H., & Segal, L. (1982). *The tactics of change: Doing therapy briefly*. San Francisco: Jossey-Bass.

Haley, J. (1973). *Uncommon therapy: The psychiatric techniques of Milton H. Erickson, M.D.* New York: Norton.

Haley, J. (1984). *Ordeal therapy: Unusual ways of changing people.* San Francisco: Jossey-Bass.

Madanes, C. (1981). *Strategic family therapy.* San Francisco: Jossey-Bass.

Madanes, C. (1984). *Behind the one-way mirror: Advances in the practice of strategic therapy.* San Francisco: Jossey-Bass.

Mazza, J. (1984). Symptom utilization in strategic therapy. *Family Process, 23*(4):487-500.

McGinnis, A.L. (1990). *The power of optimism.* San Franciso: Harper & Row.

O'Hanlon, W.H., & Weiner-Davis, M. (1989). *In search of solutions: A new direction in psychotherapy.* New York: Norton.

Schulem, B. (1988). The introduction of humor in supervision and therapy — work is depressive enough without being too serious. *Journal of Strategic and Systemic Therapies, 7*(2):49-58.

Tomm, K. (1987a). Interventive interviewing: Part I. Strategizing as a fourth guideline for the therapist. *Family Process, 26*(1):3-13.

Tomm, K. (1987b). Interventive interviewing: Part II. Reflexive questioning as a means to enable self healing. *Family Process, 26*(2):167-184.

Tomm, K. (1988). Interventive Interviewing: Part III. Intending to ask lineal, circular, strategic, or reflexive questions? *Family Process, 27*(1):1-15.

Weiner-Davis, M., de Shazer, S., & Gingerich, W. (1987). Using pretreatment change to construct a therapeutic solution: A clinical note. *Journal of Marital and Family Therapy, 13*(4):359-363.

Wernitznig, H. (1987/88). Sneaky Poo comes to stay: A bedtime story for parents to read to their children. *Dulwich Centre Newsletter,* Summer, 11-14.

White, M. (1984). Pseudo-encopresis: From avalanche to victory, from vicious to virtuous cycles. *Family Systems Medicine, 2*(2):150-160.

White, M., & Epston, D. (1990). *Narrative means to therapeutic ends.* New York: Norton.

White, M. (1990). Selected papers. Adelaide, South Australia: Dulwich Centre Publications.

SELECTED BIBLIOGRAPHY
OF ARTICLES AND BOOKS
BY THE AUTHORS

Furman, B. (1990). Glasnost therapy: Removing the barriers between client and therapist. *Family Therapy Networker*, May/June.

Furman, B., & Ahola, T. (1990). Pathways to radical relativism and impact on therapy. *Human Systems: The Journal of Systemic Consultation and Management*, 1(1):5–18.

Furman, B., & Ahola, T. (1989). The chicken and the egg: A hindsight view of therapy. *Journal of Family Therapy*, 11:217–230.

Furman, B., & Ahola, T. (1989). Adverse effects of psychotherapeutic beliefs. *Family Systems Medicine*, 7(2):183–195. Also in German (1990), Nachteilige Auswirkungen von psychotherapeutischen Annahmen. *Familiendynamik*, 15(4):288–304.

Furman, B. (1989). Giving consultation to one's parents: What is a task for? *Case Studies*, 3(1):19–23.

Furman, B., & Ahola, T. (1988). The return of the question why: The advantages of exploring pre-existing explanations. *Family Process*, 27(4):395–409.

Furman, B., & Ahola, T. (1988). The use of humor in brief therapy. *Journal of Strategic and Systemic Therapies*, 7(2):3–20

Furman, B., & Ahola, T. (1988). The seven illusions. *Family Therapy Networker*, Sept/Oct, 30–31.

Ahola, T., & Furman, B. (1990). *Juonia Juopoille: Ratkaisukeskeinen lähestymistapa päihdeongelmiin [Solutions to alchohol and drug problems]*. Helsinki: Lyhytterapia-Instituutti. Also published in Swedish (1990) under the title *Lösningar För Misbrukare*. Stockholm, Sweden: Mareld Kooperativa Bokförlag. Danish translation in press, Kopenhagen: Förlaget politisk revy.

Furman, B. (1986). *Lyhytterapia ja perheterapia: Psykiatrian uudet suuntaukset* [Brief therapy and family therapy: New directions in psychiatry]. Keuruu, Finland: Otava.

Furman, B., & Ahola, T. (1990). *Taskuvarkaat nudistileirillä: Kumous terapiamaailmassa* [Pickpockets in a nudist camp: Revolution in the world of therapy]. Helsinki: ai-ai. Also published in Swedish (1988) under the title *Ficktjuven på nudistlägret: Den systemiska revolutionen inom psykoterapin.* Helsinki: ai-ai.

INDEX